James Lind

An essay on the most effectual means of preserving the health of seamen, in the Royal Navy

Containing directions proper for all those who undertake long voyages at sea, or reside in unhealthy situations. Second Edition

James Lind

An essay on the most effectual means of preserving the health of seamen, in the Royal Navy
Containing directions proper for all those who undertake long voyages at sea, or reside in unhealthy situations. Second Edition

ISBN/EAN: 9783337730369

Printed in Europe, USA, Canada, Australia, Japan

Cover: Foto ©ninafisch / pixelio.de

More available books at **www.hansebooks.com**

AN ESSAY

ON THE

MOST EFFECTUAL MEANS

Of preserving the

HEALTH of SEAMEN,

In the ROYAL NAVY.

CONTAINING

DIRECTIONS proper for all those who undertake long Voyages at Sea, or reside in unhealthy Situations.

WITH

CAUTIONS necessary for the Preservation of such Persons as attend the Sick in Fevers.

By JAMES LIND, M. D.

Physician to the King's Hospital at Haslar, near Portsmouth;
And Fellow of the Royal College of Physicians in Edinburgh.

The SECOND EDITION, Improved and Enlarged.

Principiis Obsta.

LONDON:
Printed for D. WILSON, at Plato's Head, in the Strand.
MDCCLXII.

To the Right Honourable

GEORGE LORD EDGCUMBE,

My Lord,

I Beg Leave to prefix your Lordship's Name, as the moſt proper Introduction to this *ESSAY*, by exhibiting a Pattern of that humane Diſpoſition, which is requiſite to put in Practice the Rules contained in the following Pages.—A Diſpoſition not leſs honourable to your Lordſhip, than beneficial to the Public; and which, added to many other amiable Qualities, rendered you eſteemed by your Officers, beloved by your Men, and reſpected

respected by all, who felt the happy Influence of your Command.

That, in the Royal Navy, so laudable an Example may become the Object of universal Imitation, is the sincere Wish of,

MY LORD,

Your Lordship's most obedient,

and most humble Servant,

JAMES LIND.

THE
PREFACE.
TO THE
FIRST EDITION.

IN Times of public Tranquillity, when only smaller Ships of War are employed, and manned with sound and seasoned Sailors, their Cruises or Voyages short, and sufficient Opportunity allowed to refresh in Harbour, the Seamen in his Majesty's Service are in general, healthy.

—A

—— A ſhip of fifty or ſixty Guns, commonly buries fewer Men in three Years, than moſt Villages in *England*, containing a like Number of Inhabitants, except in a few accidental Caſes; as when a Ship upon the Coaſt of *Guinea*, or the *Weſt-Indies*, ſuffers by any extraordinary Efforts of Sickneſs, derived from Cauſes hereafter ſpecified.

But Circumſtances widely differ in the turbulent State of War, or when any Emergency requires the immediate Equipment of a large Fleet, and renders the impreſſing of Men abſolutely neceſſary. Then it is, that Sailors, returning with exhauſted Conſtitutions, from long and ſickly Voyages in the Merchants Service, and Perſons unaccuſtomed to a marine Life, as well as many naked and diſeaſed Objects dragged from the Streets and ſwept from the Priſons, are promiſcuouſly ſent on board.——Hence various Cauſes of Sickneſs in a Ship: of which, the Infection received

received from Men lately diseased, or from the tainted Rags of Jails, is none of the least.

Too close Confinement in the damp and foul Air of large Ships, Discontent, and the requisite Duty of the Service, may also create Diseases: and the Intercourse of different Ships serves often to propagate them by Contagion; especially when the Removal of the Sick on shore is inconvenient, on account of the Danger of their Desertion.—— Thus it is, that many Distempers which, in a well-aired City or Village, would affect only a few Individuals, may, in such Patients, and from their peculiar Situation in a Ship, acquire a high Degree of Virulence, and put on a contagious Disposition.

All acknowledge the Train of Diseases, to which, from the Mechanism of our Body, we are necessarily subject. And it is as manifest, that many more are produced,

duced, by fupervening external Caufes. Thus a quick Tranfition to a new Way of Life, fudden Changes of Climates, the various Inconveniencies and Hardfhips peculiar to Mariners, plainly account for many of their Difeafes. Nor is it to be doubted, but that proper Methods and Precautions might be taken to prepare and inure the Body to bear fuch fenfible Alterations, as are apt to affect the Conftitution; and that by removing, or guarding againft, other Caufes of Sicknefs, to which Sailors are expofed, the Health and Lives of many of them, who are extremely negligent in this Point, might be happily preferved.

It may be worth obferving, that the *prophylactic* or preventive Branch of medical Science does, in many Inftances, admit of as much, or even more Certainty, than the curative Part. For it would be eafy to demonftrate, that the Rules for the Prefervation of Health and Life, in many fingular and dangerous Situations, are founded on clear and self-evident Principles. They are often the natural Dictates of Sense and Appetite, approved by Reason, and established by Observation. The Advantages also resulting from such like salutary Precepts, are superior to any other; as the nauseous Dose is here avoided or abridged, and as a Medicine, which effectually prevents, deserves to be more esteemed than that which removes a Fever.—Diseases, precarious in their Event, though at last cured, impair the Constitution, render it liable to Relapses, or other subsequent Attacks; and, the Patient is necessarily afflicted, for a Time, with Infirmity and *Languor*.

With Regard to the Royal Navy, when the Men are preserved in Health, by proper Management; Courage and Activity are the certain Consequences.

To a Crew replete in Health, what Enterprize too dangerous? What Atchievement too great? Whereas a sickly Shp's Company,

Company, impotent and difpirited, have fruftrated many a well-concerted Expedition, and that Bravery, which the Enemies of our Country have not been able to vanquifh, has fallen a Sacrifice to the cruel Ravage of devouring Difeafe.

An additional Motive to excite the public Attention to this important Subject, (the Prefervation of the Health of our Seamen) is the confiderable Savings, which will thereby be made, in immenfe Sums expended by the Government, in the Article of Hofpitals, and the various Neceffaries, which are there fo amply provided for them.

If then it fhall appear probable, that by obferving a few eafy and practicable Rules here delivered, the Health and Lives of many of our Sailors may be preferved, I flatter myfelf, that this *Effay* will meet with a favourable Reception. And it is a great Pleafure to me, upon this Occafion, to addrefs

addrefs the Commanders of his Majesty's Ships of War; as I know many of them, who are no less distinguished by their Valour, than by their compassionate Care of their Men.

It gives me no small Satisfaction to observe, that since the ensuing Sheets were sent to the Press, the Government has purposed to introduce in the Royal Navy, an Allowance of portable Soup; a Regulation, on which the Service may be truly congratulated; nor is it less laudable than advantageous to the Public, and deserving from our Seamen the warmest Gratitude.

Common Humanity, indeed, ever pleads for the Afflicted, and calls for the Assistance of all, whose Abilities or Observations are capable of rescuing Mankind from Pain, and the many direful Attendants of Disease. But, surely, there are no Lives more valuable to the State, or have a better Claim to its Care,

Care, than those of the *British* Sailors, to whom this Nation, in great measure, owes its Riches, Protection, and Liberties.

What is here proposed, is chiefly founded upon Experience, and the Result of an Attention to the Diseases more peculiarly incident to the Royal Navy.

In an Affair so highly interesting, as the Lives of many of my Fellow Subjects, I shall often take Notice of Circumstances, which may be deemed too minute. But be it not forgot, that upon a due Observance of many such Circumstances, Matters of Consequence will depend. Preservatives from Sickness ought, as little as possible, to consist in Medicines, but rather in such general Precepts, as all may easily obey. A few present seeming Inconveniencies attending the Rules recommended, may be abundantly

dantly compensated by future Benefits. And I make no doubt, but Time and Use will reconcile the Men to some Things in these Sheets, if approved, which bear the Face of Novelty.

Nothing, I am afraid, has contributed more to the great Sickness of late in our Fleet, than too strict an Attachment to old Regulations and Customs. Some new Regulations are plainly wanted. But as there is no universal Medicine to be found in Nature for all Diseases, so neither is there any one particular Method, much less any single Medicine, which can afford an effectual and universal Protection against the various Maladies of Seamen.

The Means, here to be proposed, for the preserving the Health of a Ship's Company, are two-fold: and consist;

First

First, in the Methods proper to prevent the Generation of Sickness in a Ship.

Secondly, in certain Precautions to stop the Spreading of contagious Diseases, when bred.

ADVERTISEMENT

TO THE

SECOND EDITION.

THIS book was first published, soon after the commencement of the present war with France, as a plan of directions for preserving the British seamen from such distempers as prove much more fatal to their *corps*, than all the other calamities incident to them at sea. For the number of seamen in time of war, who die by shipwreck, capture, famine, fire or sword, are indeed but inconsiderable, in respect of such as are *destroyed* by the ship diseases, and by the usual maladies of intemperate climates.

The Abbé Mascas has translated this Essay into French, and it appears there was an order given by the French king that it should be distributed to both the Indies, and to all the maritime parts of his dominions.

Dr. Wind, an eminent physician in Middleburgh, has translated it into Dutch, with the addition of some judicious notes.

My public acknowledgments are also due to Dr. Moncky, physician at Amsterdam, for the honourable mention he has made of my name in his treatise, which obtained the Dutch premium as the best answer to the question proposed by the Society of sciences in Holland, relative to the diseases of seamen in voyages to the West Indies.

I have now revised these sheets, and made some additions, endeavouring to render this performance more extensively useful, not only to all seamen and passengers in ships, but also to others, more especially to many of our colonies, and factories abroad. In the second part, I have more fully enlarged on the precepts for securing such as attend sick persons against infection, which are not confined to seamen or to ships, but intended as general directions, and as a supplement to my two papers, now published, on fevers and infection.

CONTENTS.

Preface.

SECT. I.

OF preventing the Generation of Sickness, Page 1

To secure against the Introduction of Sickness in the fleet, 2

Men, after a long foreign Voyage, to be dieted with fresh Provisions and Greens, for three Weeks, 3

Landmen, suspected of the Goal Distemper, to remain fourteen Days on board the foul Tender, 5

Cloaths brought from Newgate, or other suspected Prisons, to be destroyed, 6

Men seized with the Goal, or Ship-Fever, to be immediately separated from the rest, and sent on shore, 7

A general Method of preserving the Health of Men in Guard-ships, and in all other Ships crouded with People, 7

Of draughting Men for special Services: Or the comparative Fitness of Men for different Ships and Voyages, 9

Of Diseases incident to Seamen in Northern Climates, and to Channel-Cruisers, 12

General Means of preventing these Diseases, 13

Of the Scurvy, 16

A Method of preventing the Scurvy in the Channel Fleet, ibid.

The Freshness of a Ship's Timber, sometimes the Cause of Sickness, 20

Observations relating to it, 21

To preserve the Health of the Men in Southern, and the most sickly Voyages, 23

The Company to be put upon a short Allowance of salted Flesh-Meat, 24

A Digression, *pointing out a Method of preserving at Sea, proper Vegetables,*

Pot-

Pot-herbs, &c. quite green, fresh, and succulent, for a considerable Time, 33

A Method of procuring fresh Salad, and an antiscorbutic Water, at Sea, 35

Punch made with Cream of Tartar, recommended, 36

Directions to avert Danger in extreme Intoxication, 39

Directions to recover Persons supposed to be drowned; or such as are suffocated by the noxious Vapour from a Ship's Well—And such as are struck with Lightning, 40

Directions to prevent the bad effects of Lightning on-board Ship, 42

Several necessary Preservatives of Health, 44

The first Diseases usually incident in a Southern Voyage, 47

The most frequent and fatal Distempers, 49

A Bark-Bitter recommended for Prevention, 59

Precautions to be taken upon a Ship's Arrival at a sickly Port, or in an unhealthy Season, 64

Pre-

Precautions relating to the Ship, 67

Precautions relating to the Men employed on Shore, 72

Of a most extraordinary and unwholesome Vapour, met with in Guinea, 79

Ships in Distress by Sickness, being in an unhealthy Harbour, to put to Sea for the Preservation of the Men, 81

Various Articles useful at Sea, more particularly for the Recovery of sick and weak Persons, 82

Different Methods of procuring good and wholesome Water both at Sea and Land; as also of saving fresh Water, by dressing the Ship's Provisions altogether with Sea-Water, 85

SECT. II.

*R*ULES to be observed, for putting a Stop to the Spreading of putrid and contagious Diseases, 94

Rules respecting the Place allotted for the Sick, 101

Rules respecting the Diseased, 103

An

An approved Method of purifying the Air in a Ship, during a Sickness among the Men, 105

Rules to be observed for the Security of the Surgeons, the Attendants on the Sick, and the rest of the Ship's Company, 106

The Manner of cleansing and purifying a Ship, or any other Place, from Infection, 114

Of Hospitals, 120

Superior Advantages of Seamen in the Royal Navy, to those in the Merchants Service, 124

APPENDIX.

Containing Directions concerning the Method of treating acute Diseases in hot Climates, 127

Also the comparative Quantities of Heat and Cold in different Places and Latitudes, as measured by the same Instrument, 133

POSTSCRIPT.

The Diseases, that are most frequent and fatal to Mariners, shewn from an Abstract of the Cases of 5743 Sick Seamen, 141

ADDEN-

ADDENDA.

Page 42, line 15, after *immersed*, read, *up to the chin*.

Page ibid. line 26, after *the veins &c.* read, *and dashing a large bucketful, or two, of cold water on his face, naked stomach, or thighs; by the shock of which many have instantly recovered from the danger of being suffocated by the vapour from the ship's well, and other noxious damps.*

Page 90, line 26, after *clean vessels or casks*, read, *If all vessels, commonly used at sea for boiling on the fire, were furnished with such a head, the double advantage not only of saving much fuel, but a great quantity of water, would be reaped. Thus, if the barley-water, gruels &c. for the sick, which are made with fresh water, be boiled in this manner, all the water which would otherwise be expended by boiling away, would then be saved; and nothing further is required than that the pots or saucepans be somewhat larger than at present used, because they ought then never to be filled above one half or three quarters full, and the cover must not be so tight, but that the cook may easily remove it at all times, either to inspect into the condition of what is cooking, or to stir about such materials in the pot, as are apt to rise up, or boil over, which I find oatmeal to be the only article of ships provisions that does. The cook will soon learn what small quantity of fuel is necessary to keep such pots boiling, and the trouble of a more constant attendance to prevent the boiling over, will be fully rewarded, by saving two of the most important articles at sea, fuel and water.*

As the evaporation from water is as the squares of its surface, hence so much the wider the iron pots are made, which were before recommended for the sides of the grates, the more fresh water will be obtained.

AN ESSAY

ON THE

Most effectual Means of preserving the Health of Seamen in the Royal Navy.

SECT. I.

Of preventing the Breeding of Sickness.

IN the Equipment of a Fleet there are two Sorts of Men from whom Sickness may be apprehended, *viz.* Sailors imprest after a long Voyage from the *East* or *West-Indies*, or the Coast of *Guinea*; and such idle Fellows as are picked from the Streets or the Prisons.

The former are often deeply tainted with scorbutic and other Disorders, which usually break out upon a longer Confinement and Fatigue at Sea. The Constitution might, in this Case, by proper Care, be surprisingly soon restored, and the Men duly prepared for another Voyage.

From the latter Set of Men, there is Danger of communicating Infection to the whole Fleet. That there is a Disease of a contagious Nature, the Produce of Filth, Rags, Poverty, and a polluted Air, which subsists always in a greater or less Degree in crowded Prisons, and in all nasty, low, damp, unventilated Habitations loaded with putrid animal Steams, is now well known, and has been too often fatally experienced, by taking such contaminated Persons into our Ships.

With Deference then to better qualified Judges, I would beg Leave to suggest, that the proper Method to be taken to secure the future Health of the imprest Sailors, and to obviate the Mischiefs which might accrue from diseased Landmen, seems to be this.

In the usual Descriptions of imprest Men taken by the regulating Captains, it would be proper to insert their former Way of Life,

the

the Place of their late Residence, their present State of Health; and, with regard to Sailors, the Length and Healthfulness of their last Voyage. If, in Consequence of this Report, those who are just arrived from a long and sickly Voyage, were directly allowed fresh Provisions, and especially a sufficient Quantity of Greens, in *lieu* of salted and other Meats, a Diet of this Sort continued for at least three Weeks, would, in all Probability, sufficiently cleanse and restore their Constitution, and fit them for immediate Service.

A different Method may be necessary to be taken with imprest Landmen. A Guard-ship is usually stationed at the *Nore*, to receive those who are taken up in *London*. But Experience has shewn how fatal she has often proved to the Health and Lives of many Seamen; and that this Ship has become a Seminary of Contagion to the whole Fleet. One diseased Person from the Street, or Cloaths from a Prison, have often conveyed Infection on board, which it has been extremely difficult afterwards to get quit of. For the confined and corrupted Air in a large crowded Ship, greatly favours the spreading of this Contagion, and the Exertion of its utmost Malignity. From this Source, the Environs of *Portsmouth* and *Plymouth* have more than once been annoyed with an almost pestilential Contagion, which certain Regulations might, in all Probability, have effectually prevented *.

To

---

* This has hitherto been the most fatal and general Cause of Sickness in the Royal Navy, especially on the first fitting out of the Ships. In the Commencement of the present War, the Seeds of Infection were carried from the Guard-ships into our Squadrons, to all Quarters of the World, and particularly to *North America*, by the large Fleets which sailed thither: And the Mortality, thence occasioned, was greater than by all other Diseases or Means of Death put together.

After the receiving Guard-ships were repeatedly purified, by the most proper Orders and Methods for that Purpose, fresh Draughts of imprest Men still continued the Infection, in Opposition to all the Care taken by the Officers, and their utmost Vigilance and Attention to keep these Ships sweet, well-aired, and clean: Nor could it be otherwise; for the purest Air cannot cleanse Rags from Contagion. I have known a thousand Men confined together in one Guard-ship, some hundreds of whom had neither a Bed, nor so much as a Change of Linen; I have seen many of these brought into *Haslar* Hospital, in the same Cloaths and Shirts they had on, when pressed several Months before. In this Case, it was impossible to prevent the Generation or Progress of Disease. The fatal Mischief lurked in their tainted Apparel, and Rags; and by these was conveyed into other Ships. A late Instance is sufficiently known, where the polluted Cloaths of Prisoners, brought from *Newgate*, and other unclean Places, have infected and destroyed the Judges

To prevent the Communication of the Infection, a Tender might be appointed in the River, to receive such Men only as the Regulating-Captains should direct. There, the most ragged and suspicious Persons, whether prest at Sea, or on Shore, should remain for at least

on the Bench, and others, in an open Court: And still greater Danger may be apprehended from such Materials in a Ship.

If the Captains of those Guard-ships had ordered a Supply of Bedding, and such Seamen's Cloaths as are commonly called *Slops*, to all such imprest and transferred Men as were in want of them; it is said, they would have encumbered their Ship-books so much with *Slop* Articles, as to have rendered it difficult for them to have passed their Accounts. This I believe to be the candid Matter of Fact. The Means of obviating these Difficulties, and of averting in future Equipments, during a warm Press, the Danger that is to be apprehended, I must leave to better Judges, and my Superiors: Mean while, with due Submission, I shall suggest the following Expedient. If the Seamen in his Majesty's Service were put into an uniform Sea-Habit, with some little moveable Badges, or Variations (if judged necessary) by which it might be known to what Ship they belong; each Man would at first go clean and neatly cloathed on board his Majesty's Ships; and by the proper Care of the Officers, in frequently inspecting their Apparel, be kept so constantly: And all the Inconveniencies of serving *Slops*, and the Abuse of some Seamen in selling and destroying them, might, perhaps, be effectually prevented.

fourteen

fourteen Days, where their old Cloaths might be deſtroyed, and new ones given them; and their Perſons being well purified and cleanſed, they would thus be prevented from carrying Rags, Filth, and Infection on board the King's Ships.

The Precaution of deſtroying the Cloaths of all ſuch who are brought from *Newgate*, or other ſuſpected Places, ought not to be neglected; becauſe, although fourteen Days may be a ſufficient Time to diſcover whether a Perſon is free from the Taint, yet we cannot preciſely determine what Time may be neceſſary to purge their Apparel from this Contagion. Woollen Cloaths, in particular, are diſpoſed to retain it a conſiderable Time.

It may be proper further to obſerve, that when a Tender arrives, with impreſt Men, at the *Nore*, from any Part of *Great-Britain* or *Ireland*, who, having been long confined, under cloſe-ſhut *Hatchways* *, during bad Weather, or in Summer Time, may be ſuppoſed to have ſuffered by the polluted Air †, in ſuch a

---

* The Openings or Doors by which they deſcend from one Deck or Floor of a Ship to another.

† This may be known by ſeveral complaining of Shiverings, Pains of the Breaſt, with Cough, too often miſtaken for Fits of an Ague, or common Colds, and others of a Head-ach, accompanied with a low Fever.

Case, the Sick ought to be sent into a Lazaretto, Hospital, or well-aired Place on Shore; and the rest of the Men refreshed by good Air, but especially to have their Persons well purified, and supplied with clean Slops. If it should happen that this Vessel is truly infected, she ought to be purified in the Manner proposed in the second Section of this Essay.

In Time of War, the Guard-ships become often excessively crowded with prest, transferred Men, &c. which the Exigency of the Service requires. At this Season, the Officers must be particularly careful in the Article of Cleanliness in the Ship. For this Purpose, the Cloaths of the Men ought frequently to be inspected, to prevent their selling of them; and thereby reducing themselves to all the Inconveniencies attending the Want of a sufficient Quantity of clean Apparel: Nakedness, Sloth, and Filth greatly contributing to the Production of Diseases. The Men and *Hammocks* * ought every Morning, in fair Weather, to be sent upon Deck, when the Gun-ports should be opened, and the lower Decks well scraped and washed; mean while such a Number of Hammocks should be scrubbed and cleaned, that every Hammock in the Ship may have undergone this Ope-

* The hanging Beds of Seamen.

ration

ration at least once a Month. In bad or moist Weather, the lower Decks must only be scraped and swept. When the Weather will permit, Fires of dried Wood must be used between Decks, lighted in Iron Kettles, or large Tubs, filled partly with Shot and Sand. The burning Wood may be occasionally sprinkled with some Resin, or Bits of Rope, dipt in Pitch and Tar. These Fires must be carried into all the different Parts of the Ship, that Safety will permit; I mean, the *Berths* * of the Men. During the Continuance of rainy, moist Weather, the Ship ought, twice a Day, to be fumigated with the Steam of Pitch or Tar, raised by a hot Iron; and, upon the Return of good Weather, be thoroughly cleansed, as above directed, with the Addition of having the Beams, &c. where the Men lay, washed with warm Vinegar. Nor must this important Direction be omitted, that the Air, both by Night and Day, be renewed by the incessant working of the *Ventilators*.—— By such Methods duly practised, not only Guard-ships, crowded with Men, but all other Ships, will probably continue healthy.

* A Term used at Sea for the Place where the Men eat and sleep.

As raw Sailors, and unseasoned Marines, are often the Occasion of great Sickness in Fleets, during their long Cruises and Voyages, I must beg Leave further to suggest—That the draughting of Men for special Services, if it can be done, could not fail of having a good Effect in the Service. The Rank of the Captain, and the present Fitness of the Ship, are not, perhaps, always the chief Things to be considered; as the Condition of a Ship's Company, who are to be sent upon a distant Expedition, is a Circumstance which must needs influence, in a great Measure, the Success of the Voyage.

We observe a just Distinction made in the Army between Veterans, and new-raised Levies. But the Change of Life, from the Civil to the Military, is not so great, nor so affecting to the Constitution, as a Change to the Marine Manner of Living. If Volunteer-Landmen, and new-raised Marines, were at first incorporated with Seamen, on Board armed Vessels, Tenders, and small Ships of War only, it should seem that, by this Means, they would not only become good Sailors in a shorter Time, but would gradually acquire a stronger Constitution, fitted for the Marine Duty, without running the Risk of Sickness at first, or of Laziness and Indolence afterwards, from want of Exercise, these

small

small and well-aired Ships being always the most healthful, and most employed. Whereas, on the contrary, it is observable, that large Ships, on first fitting out, especially the capital ones, are more liable to Sickness, even when lying at *Spithead*, or in Harbour; so that the Draughts made into them, should be of seasoned healthy Men from other Ships, and of such Landmen as have been somewhat inured to the Sea.

If it be said, that the large Ships, when manned with a seasoned Crew, are observed to be very healthy; yet there is more Caution seemingly requisite to prevent Sickness being introduced among so great a Number of Men, than in Ships of a smaller Complement.

When a Squadron is fitted out for a long and dangerous Voyage, no Method would, perhaps, promise greater Security for future Health, than to make Draughts chiefly of such Men, from the smaller Frigates, as had been for some Time healthy and seasoned to the Sea; including in these, as many as offer of such Sailors who had been accustomed to the Climate. This I am obliged to take Notice of, as a very different Method is often followed. When there is Choice of Men, the Captains generally prefer the most able-bodied

raw

raw young Fellows. But it has been evinced, by fatal Experience, that such vigorous Constitutions are more liable than others to be cut off by violent Fevers in hot Climates; nothing is more common than for such Ships to lose their best Men. Whereas many hardened veteran Sailors are sometimes to be met with, who enjoy a better State of Health in the *West-Indies* than in *Europe*, having been long seasoned and inured to that Climate, either in the King's, or in the Merchant's Service.

A Crew of such Men not only carry out a Constitution suited to the Climate, but, being prepossessed in its Favour, are entirely void of those Apprehensions, and that Dread of Sickness, which prove hurtful to unseasoned *Europeans*.

Large Men of War ought to have as many as offer of these Hands: And, in the Course of the Voyage, it might be proper to have them recruited from the smaller Ships, as all new Sailors will continue much healthier, and become sooner seasoned in small Cruisers.

What I have thus far proposed, I am sensible may be often found incompatible with the immediate Exigencies of the Service; and is, with due Deference, submitted to the Consideration of superior Judges, and of those who have the Superintendance of the medical Marine Department.——I now pass on to what is more properly the Subject of this Essay, *viz.* To propose the most effectual Methods of preserving the Health of the Men at Sea, and of preventing the various Distempers incident to them in different Climates, and which proceed from their peculiar Circumstances and Situation.

I shall begin with such Maladies as are usual in northern Climates, and among the Channel Cruisers.

Though an intense Degree of Cold, if the Air is at the same Time pure and dry, is productive of few Diseases, when Seamen are sufficiently cloathed, and kept in due Exercise, yet such a State of Air is not often met with at Sea in northern Latitudes, nor by our Channel Cruisers in the Winter.—— The Season is then, for the most Part, unsettled, cloudy, moist, and rainy, and the Men must necessarily undergo an extraordinary Fatigue, during the inconstant and tempestuous Weather which they are almost continually engaged with. The usual Consequences, are
Colds

Colds, accompanied with feverish and inflammatory Symptoms, and especially rheumatic, pleuritic, and peripneumonic Complaints. These latter Cases require plentiful Evacuations, chiefly Blood-letting; by the early and free Use of which, many Consumptions, as as also chronic Rheumatisms, an afflicting Ailment to old Sailors, may be prevented.

Now as most Disorders, especially catarrhal Fevers, usual at this Season, are probably owing to a Stoppage of Perspiration; hence, whatever promotes that necessary Evacuation, seems to promise the most certain Protection against these Evils. And, for this Purpose, I would in the first Place, by Way of Diet, recommend a very simple Preservative; it is, the free Use of Eschalot, Garlic, or Onions. The two former are put up with the Surgeon's Necessaries, but are so very cheap, that they may be afforded by the Purser, in *lieu* of the Savings of Oatmeal. Instead of Burgou, Water-gruel might be served in a Morning to the Men, with a proper Quantity of Eschalot, Onions, Leeks, or Garlic, boiled in it. This will be found as wholesome a Mess as can well be contrived for Seamen at that Season. It is an antiscorbutic, as also a tepid, relaxing, perspirative Diluent; and Food possessed of these Properties, is the proper Antidote to

the

the hurtful Influences of cold bad Weather at Sea.

Most of the Channel Cruisers have a Quantity of Brandy put on Board to be served to the Men, when the Small-beer is expended; but there is often Occasion for it sooner; because, during a violent Storm of Wind, or in bad Weather, or when the People are kept constantly wet and chill, and undergo an uncommon Degree of Fatigue, Small-beer does not sufficiently support their Strength and Spirits. Upon this Occasion, an Allowance of half their quantity of Small-beer, and a Quantity of Brandy, equal to the Remainder, would be found very beneficial. It should be mixed up in the following Manner: To a Pint of Small-beer, add a Quartern, or fourth Part of a Pint of Brandy; let it be sweetened with Molasses, and acidulated with Vinegar, so as to be made palatable. This is a celebrated Beverage in the *Russian* Army, where it is called *Ashbetten*; no Regiment marches without carrying a Cask of it along with them: And it is by this corroborative Drink, the Men are supported, and enabled to undergo their long and fatiguing Marches. They, indeed use Honey instead of Molasses; and their Physicians have lately made some Improvements in the Composition, by an Infusion

sion of Gentian, and other aromatic Bitters in the Spirit, which would seem, however, to be of no great Consequence.

This Draught will be found much wholesomer than un-diluted Spirits; the serving of which to the Men, towards the End of their long Cruises, contributes often to excite general and fatal Scurvies in the Fleet. The Fermentation occasioned by the Molasses, or Honey, and the Addition of Vinegar, or, in its Stead, Cream of Tartar, as shall hereafter be mentioned, will in some Measure serve to obviate that, and some other Maladies usual in these Cruises.

But, at the same time, it is necessary to observe——That dry warm Cloathing and Bedding, are of the greatest Consequence in Winter, and without which, other Means of preserving Health will have little Effect. Every Man should be obliged to furnish himself with at least two Flannel Under-Jackets, an Article which ought to be added to the Purser's Slops. They are generally the most naked and ragged Fellows who are attacked with the Winter Diseases. When the Hammocks are carried up to Quarters, they ought always to be covered with a painted or tarred Canvas, kept for the Purpose; and it ought to be

particularly

particularly remembered, that humid Cloaths and Bedding are frequently a leading Cause of Sickness in a Ship.

The Scurvy is a Disease common in the Winter and Spring, and very fatal to Seamen in the Channel Cruisers. But ample Directions have already been given for the Prevention and effectual Cure of this Calamity.*

I cannot, however, omit taking Notice of one Thing: When large Squadrons of Men of War are kept constantly employed in the Channel Service, the Length of their Cruises, generally from ten to thirteen Weeks, often occasions a great Sickness; and of late a greater Mortality has been observed, than could well be expected in such a healthy Climate. When so long a Continuance at Sea is indispensably requisite, the following has been proposed as a most excellent and effectual Expedient, to preserve the Health of a Fleet.

One of the Press-Tenders might be ordered out once a Fortnight from *Plymouth*, to repair

---

* Dr. *Lind*'s Treatise on the Scurvy, especially Chap. III. Part 2; where many more Directions concerning the Preservation of Seamen, both in Health and Sickness, are delivered; and which is deemed unnecessary to repeat.

to the Rendezvous or Station of the Squadron, loaded with live Cattle and Greens, to be ſerved to the Men by the Purſer, in *lieu* of their ſalted Meats. The Men on Board of her ſhould have the Privilege of carrying out, for their private Advantage, all Manner of Roots, Fruits, and Vegetables, to be ſold at a reaſonable Rate in the Fleet: By ſuch Means, a Market of Greens and Fruits might conſtantly be kept by Suttlers, who ſhould be only prohibited the Sale of Spirits. Onions, Leeks, Shallots, Turneps, Cabbage, Carrots, Apples, freſh ſoft Bread, Cyder, Lemons and Oranges; or even the moſt common Herbs in their Seaſon, which grow in great Plenty wild in the Fields about *Plymouth*; ſuch as Dandelion, Water-creſſes, Brooklime, and the like ſovereign Antiſcorbutics, would prove a high Refreſhment to the Men; and would ſoon be bought up by them either with Money, or, if that is wanting, in Exchange of their Savings of ſalt Meat and Biſcuit, which are commonly ſold to the Purſer for ready Money, which is expended in pernicious Drams.

The Run of the Storeſhip, or Tender, from *Plymouth* or *Ireland*, to the Fleet, will ſeldom, with a fair Wind, prove above forty-eight Hours. Many Sorts of Greens may be preſerved for any Length of Time, by a Method afterwards

afterwards to be described. But there are some Articles which the Suttlers ought to be obliged at all Times to carry out, and be provided with, in Proportion to the Rate of the Ship, upon Pain of forfeiting their Licence. These are either the Rob of Lemons, or Juice of Oranges;* and the Juices of the above-mentioned common antiscorbutic Herbs, which being mixed with a sixth Part of Brandy, will remain good for many Months.

It is hardly to be supposed that any Man, who has the least Tendency to a Scurvy, would not willingly part with a Piece of salt Beef, or a Pound or two of Biscuit, to purchase these obvious Means of Health, and a Reprieve from dying of a most painful and loathsome Disease. By a proper established Regulation of this Sort, not only some thousand Lives might be preserved; but the Ships would be enabled longer to keep the Seas, and not be often under the Necessity of quitting their Station, on account of a sickly, dying, and dispirited Crew.†

I shall

---

* See Dr. *Lind*'s Treatise on the Scurvy, Page 162.

† The remarkable good Effects of supplying the Fleet with fresh Provisions and Greens at Sea, and in the Bay of *Biscay*, have now been fully experienced in the grand Fleet under Sir *Edward Hawke* and others, Anno 1759, 1760.

I shall now conclude this Part of my Subject, with some Directions which may be of Use to particular Persons, in their cold Winter Cruises.

The most proper Spirit a Man can well use by way of a Cordial Dram, at this Season, is Garlic Brandy. He will find a much less Quantity of it, than of the pure Spirit warm his Stomach; and it will keep the Breast, Skin, and Kidneys, free from Obstructions. But here it may be worth while to subjoin a Caution, which is, that when a Man is almost chilled to Death by the excessive Cold, as I have known some by falling asleep in their Watch upon Deck, a Dram of any Spirit often proves instantly fatal. In this State he ought immediately to be put to Bed, and to swallow a Draught of some warm thin Drink, such as warm Water, Water-gruel, Sage-tea, or the like; and afterwards the distilled Spirit will prove less dangerous, and more beneficial, in restoring Warmth. Private Messes will reap Benefit in cold rainy Weather, by the Use of Sage, Sassafras, or a few toasted

1760, &c. by which Means our Sailors were preserved in the most perfect State of Health. But I shall have Occasion to give a more particular Account of this elsewhere.

Juniper

Juniper Berries, infused as Tea, with the Addition of a small Quantity of Garlic Brandy.

It may be of further Use to observe in this Climate, it is not the Degree of Cold in the Air which affects Health so much, as the sudden Changes from Heat to Cold, or from Cold to Heat; *also* the Dampness of Air—And that a Man will not be near so subject to take Cold when he is wet upon Deck, and using Exercise, as when afterwards he goes below Deck, and sits long at Rest in his wet Cloaths; and especially when he sleeps in them, or in a damp Bed. Nor will he at any Time be so liable to be affected in his Health by the Weather, if, before going upon Deck, he either eats somewhat, or drinks a little of the *Aſhbetten*, with a Bit of Biscuit, as he would be if the Stomach was quite empty.

One Cause sometimes of general Sickness, we must not here omit to mention. This is the Freshness of a Ship's Timbers: A Vapour constantly exhaling from the Wood may be felt, and is often seen by Candle-light in a well illuminated Ship.——It appears sometimes like a thin Mist, and at other Times like a luminous Stream. A prevailing Dampness is likewise evident in the Mould and Rust with which every Thing liable to either

ther is affected. It produces ill-conditioned irregular Fevers, accompanied with a Diarrhœa and anomalous Symptoms. These bad Consequences, it is much easier to prevent in the Dock-yard, than after the Ship is built: For, notwithstanding repeated Fires made to dry the Timbers, this Sweating of the Wood will continue for some Months, in a cold Country. Fumigating the Ship frequently, when at Sea, with the Steam of Tar or Pitch, may, perhaps, be found to correct, in some Measure, this pernicious Vapour; which is experienced to be attended with fewer bad Consequences in small well-aired Vessels, than in larger Ships. It is certain that very large new-built damp Men of War, are not altogether so proper for long and sickly Voyages, as those which are dry and well seasoned.*

When

---

* This Article not sufficiently attended to, well deserves Consideration. Experience, the Test of Truth, confirms the Inconvenience which Seamen suffer from the Vapours which exhale in a recent built Ship.

Whether the Exhalations from the sappy Wood operate otherwise than as simple Moisture, may admit of some Conjecture. In many Instances where the Smell cannot distinguish the Presence of any Effluvia, they will, however, exert no inconsiderable Influence. Thus, Turners, in working the Wood of the Manchaneel-Tree, would be severely affected, did they not securely guard against its Virus. The *Halitus* of a Field

of

When the Service demands any formidable Succours to be sent abroad, the *Mediterranean* seems to enjoy that happy Mediocrity of Climate to which such damp Ships might be, to the greatest Advantage, appropriated; for a Climate subject to a moist Air or Atmosphere, like our own, or that of the Channel, would protract the Seasoning of the Wood, as the Extreme of the torrid Zone would also have its Inconveniencies. What still adds to the Prejudice of the Men, and may be a needful Caution to all, is the preposterous Custom of washing the Decks after Sun-set. For, in whatever Country or Season this Method is pursued, it cannot fail of being greatly detrimental to the Seamen's Healths.

of Poppies has been known to induce a sleepy Disposition in the By-stander. The Exhalations of *Fraxinella*, and some other Plants, are said to be luminous in the warmer Countries in a very dry and calm Season: And the celebrated *Van Swieten*, in the early Part of his Life, suffered, repeatedly, a temporary Loss of Memory, from the Vicinity of a Plant to him. Vapours from Wood, especially when inclosed as in a Ship, may, besides their common relaxing Quality, convey Indisposition peculiar to their respective Natures. This by Way of Speculation.

I have lately observed, that Ships built of dry seasoned Wood, and especially where Wood Fires are often burnt betwixt Decks, are exempt, by these means, from Sickness.

For

For the Preservation of the Crew in a southern Voyage, Methods very different from what have been directed, will be found requisite. And as in these Voyages, on account of their Length, Variety of Climates, and the unhealthy Harbours Ships often put into, they incur a greater Risk of Sickness, and are with more Difficulty recruited than in *England*, therefore I shall treat this Part of my Subject at greater Length. But before I proceed to the Diseases incident to the Men in those Climates, it may be proper to premise some general Directions for their Preservation.

In an intended Voyage to the Coast of *Guinea*, the *East* or *West Indies*, the first Point of Consequence to the future Healths of the Men, seems to be to make such a Change in the Diet or Ship's Provisions, as may prepare the Body for the Alteration it must necessarily undergo, by passing from a cold to a warm Climate.——Every one's Experience must convince him, that both the Appetite and Digestion are considerably impaired in hot Weather. And it is the same in sultry Climates.

Instinct has taught the Natives between the Tropics to live chiefly on a vegetable Diet of Grains,

Grains, Roots, and fubacid Fruits; with Plenty of thin diluting Liquors. Whereas a full animal Diet, and tenacious Malt Liquors, are found to be better adapted to the Conftitution in our own, and other northern Countries. We obferve the Sailors in Winter, and efpecially fuch of them as vifit the *Greenland* Seas,* to be remarkable for a voracious Appetite, and a ftrong Digeftion of hard falted Meats, and the coarfeft Fare. But the fame Men, when fent to the *Weft Indies*, become foon fenfible of a Decay of Appetite, and find a full, grofs, falted Diet pernicious to Health.——It is, indeed, a Truth evinced by moft fatal Experience, that their devouring of large Quantities of Flefh Meats, and ufing the fame heavy obdurate Food in the *Weft Indies*, or upon the Coaft of *Guinea*, and in other warm Countries, as they were accuftomed to at home, have proved the Deftruction of many thoufand *Englifh* in thofe Climates.

The firft Step then to be taken, with a View to preferve the Health of a Squadron of Ships bound on fuch Voyages, would feem to be to diminifh the Quantity of falt Flefh Provifions. This becomes the more neceffary in fuch a Voyage, as the Men are, for the moft

* See the Bifhop of *Bergen*'s Hiftory of *Norway*, Vol. II. p. 271.

Part, put to short Allowance of Water.—— Now nothing can be more pernicious to a Ship's Company, than a full Diet of salted Beef and Pork, and at the same Time a small Quantity of Water. This is productive of scorbutic and many other Diseases, fatal at Sea, which no other Measure can avert, but a Diminution of the Government's Allowance of Beef and Pork, in Proportion to their Scarcity of Water. There remains another very material Objection against a full Diet of salted Flesh in hot Climates. It is this; that no Beef or Pork can possibly be preserved, by Sea-salt, free from a Taint or a Degree of Putrefaction, as evidently appears by the greenish Streaks in the Fat.—This might possibly be prevented by the Addition of a little Nitre in salting, whose Virtue is allowed to be proportionably enforced in the warmer Latitudes. But such Considerations being foreign to my present Purpose, I shall only observe, that as almost all Diseases in hot Climates are thought to be of a putrid Nature, so Flesh, which has a putrid Tendency, cannot fail, in some measure, of contributing to their Production.

There are not wanting Instances of the good Effects attending this Method of putting the Ship's Company, in long Voyages, upon a very a very short Allowance of salt Meats. The following is too much to the Purpose to be omitted, as it seems to demonstrate the Utility of the Measure, by a comparative Trial, at different Times, of its Effects.

In the last War, the Men belonging to the *Sheerness*, bound to the *East Indies*, apprehensive of Sickness in so long a Voyage, petitioned the Captain not to oblige them to take up their salt Provisions, but rather to permit them to live upon the other Species of their Allowance. Captain *Palliser* ordered, that they should be served with salt Meat only once a Week, *viz*. Beef one Week, and Pork the other. The Consequence was, that after a Passage of five Months and one Day, the *Sheerness* arrived at the *Cape of Good Hope*, without having so much as one Man sick on board. As the Use of *Sutton*'s Pipes had been then newly introduced into the King's Ships, the Captain was willing to ascribe Part of such an uncommon and remarkable Healthfulness, in so long a Run, to their beneficial Effects: But it was soon discovered, that, by the Neglect of the Carpenter, the Cock of the Pipes had been all this while kept shut. This Ship remained in *India* some Months, where none of the Men, excepting the Boats Crews, had the Benefit of going

going on Shore; notwithstanding which, the Crew continued to enjoy the moſt perfect State of Health. They were, indeed, well ſupplied there with freſh Meat.

On leaving that Country, knowing they were to ſtop at the *Cape of Good Hope*, and truſting to a quick Paſſage, and to the Abundance of Refreſhments to be had there, they eat their full Allowance of ſalt Meats, during a Paſſage of only ten Weeks; and it is to be remarked, the Air-pipes were now open. The Effect of this was, that when they arrived at the *Cape*, twenty of them were afflicted, in a moſt miſerable Manner, with ſcorbutic and other Diſorders. Theſe, however, were ſpeedily recovered on Shore by the Land Refreſhments.

Being now thoroughly ſenſible of the beneficial Effects of eating, in thoſe ſouthern Climates, as little ſalt Meat as poſſible, when at Sea, they unanimouſly agreed, in their Voyage home from the *Cape*, to refrain from their too plentiful Allowance of ſalted Fleſh. And thus the *Sheerneſs* arrived at *Spithead*, with her full Complement of 160 Men in perfect Health, and with unbroken Conſtitutions; having, in this Voyage of fourteen Months and fifteen Days, buried but one Man, who died in a Salivation for the Pox.

I have been told, that, according to the Regulations made for the Sick in the *French* Service, every Squadron, confisting of a certain Number of Ships, is provided with a Tender, to carry out Neceffaries for the Difeafed. The principle Articles are, live Stock, Flour for frefh Bread, Wine, &c. The frefh animal Provifions muft needs be of great Benefit to the Difeafed, though a larger Quantity of them be more indifpenfably neceffary both in the *French* and *Spanifh* Fleets, than in ours, becaufe the *Englifh*, in medical Practice, do not permit the Ufe of Flefh Soups in Fevers and other acute Diftempers, which the *French* and *Spanifh* Practitioners do.* Thefe Flefh Soups, when required at Sea, might occafionally be

---

* The *French* Allowance for their Sick, is faid to be eighteen Ounces of foft new-baked Bread, and Three-fourths of a *French* Pint of Wine a Day. They carry out Fowls of all Sorts, Bullocks, Sheep, Kids, Eggs, &c. which are diftributed to the Patients according to the Direction of the Surgeon. Their other Neceffaries are pretty much the fame with thofe furnifhed to *Englifh* Men of War, *viz.* Rice, Barley, Sugar, Tea, Prunes, Raifins, Vinegar, Spices of all Sorts; alfo Butter, Oil of Olive, &c.—We indeed have, perhaps, a better Affortment of preferved Fruits, which are extremely ufeful, fuch as Tamarinds, Currants, preferved Ginger, &c.

prepared

prepared at any Time of a portable Soup, which the Shins, the Necks, Hearts, and other Offal of the Cattle, killed at the Victualling Office, might supply. The portable Soup of Mutton, as less viscid (which Viscidity, indeed, Dilution will correct) or a Junction of both, might, occasionally, give it an acceptable Variety and Relish to sick and delicate Stomachs.

Besides the Satisfaction which would arise in common, from conferring Benefits on the Sick, the most divine of Charities, the Advantages, which those in a convalescent or recruiting State would derive from this Establishment, would abundantly recompence to the State, the apparent additional Expence, as the Preservation of its Naval Subjects would, in the End, prove the most frugal Plan.

This refreshing Sustenance, and, I may add, inspiring Cordial, on the most important Occasions in our Navy, has been long an Article among the lamented Wants, amidst the acknowledged Care and Humanity that the several honourable Boards of Marine Department have variously exercised.

Fermented Bread too, from its being sooner subdued, and assimilated into Nourishment by the weakened digestive Powers, as well as

on

on account of the Inability of Scorbutics to chew a harder Subſtance, might be very advantageouſly allowed the Sick. Nor could the Quantity conſumed by them, though daily made aboard, be any Inconvenience to the neceſſary Oeconomy and Buſineſs of the Ship. An Addition to the Leaven of a little *Caſtile* Soap diſſolved in Water, makes a Bread of the moſt eaſy Digeſtion.

Wine has likewiſe its Merits: It is found in many Fevers, eſpecially towards their Decline, to exceed, by far, the Shop medicinal Cordials. Add to this, that when the Fever is entirely gone, it proves the beſt and quickeſt Reſtorative which a Sailor can have at Sea. Rum, or other diſtilled Spirits, in whatever Manner diluted or acidulated, do not, in ſuch Caſes, produce the like Effects. It will alſo appear in the Sequel, that the Uſe of Wine becomes an excellent Means of Preſervation againſt the Infection of contagious Diſeaſes in a Ship. To anſwer theſe ſalutary Purpoſes, I would adviſe, that, before the Stock of *Madeira*, *Canary*, or other Wine, is quite expended, ſome Caſks ſhould be reſerved for the Uſe of the Sick in the Voyage. This may be iſſued to them at proper Seaſons, as the Surgeon may direct, in *lieu* of Rum, or whatever Spirits are in Uſe at the Time.

I am of Opinion, that proper Regulations for preventing the Abuse, and improving the Benefit that may be derived from such vinous and spirituous Liquors as are allowed to the Men, cannot fail, at all Times, to have a very remarkable Influence on the Health of the Crew. The Abuse of these Liquors, more especially the swallowing down large Quantities of undiluted Spirits, is of the most fatal Consequence in every Climate, and has been the Bane of many thousand Mariners; while, on the other hand, it is most certain, that by proper Management, these noxious Draughts might be converted into a sovereign Remedy in unwholsome Climates. This, the Sea-Officers, who drink more of them than the common Men, daily experience. Observation has indeed sufficiently instructed us, that distilled Spirits, well diluted and acidulated, and used in a moderate Quantity, are wholsome, and proper for healthy labouring Men in hot Weather. Somewhat is requisite to support the Strength of such People, and perhaps Punch is the most salutary Liquor that can be contrived to answer this Purpose; besides its immediate cooling, refreshing, and invigorating Quality, it is, in the Whole, well adapted to prevent the Diseases arising from hot and moist Weather, and the Tendency to Corruption in the animal Juices, which is thence supposed to be induced.

If the *West Indians* could fall upon a Method of making such large Quantities, at a Time, of the Rob, or inspissated Juice of Lemons or Limes,* as would reduce them to a low Price, Mariners, and all other Inhabitants of the Torrid Zone, might then be supplied with a noble Preservative of Health, in sultry unhealthful Climates. One of the greatest Physicians † of the *Indies* makes the following Remark: " The most knowing Practitioners " in *India* place greater Confidence in Le" mons against the malignant Diseases, pesti" lential Fevers, &c. of the Country, than " in costly Bezoar or Theriac. For my own " Part, says he, I affirm, that in my Practice " there, I found more Benefit from them, " than from any one simple Remedy."

Syrup of Lemons ought always to be put in the Surgeon's Medicine Chest, and be occasionally prepared and renewed in a sufficient Quantity, at every Port, where these Fruits are cheap and in Season. Orange Juice, an excellent Succedaneum from Lemons, may be preserved, during the Course of the longest Voyage, in the following Manner. Care must first be taken to squeeze only sound Fruit, as

---

* See Dr. *Lind*'s Treatise on the Scurvy, second Edition, p. 162.

† Bontius de Medicina Ind.

a tainted Orange will endanger the spoiling of the whole; the expressed Juice must be depurated by standing a few Days, or filtrated till it is pretty clear; then it is to be put into small Bottles, none of them containing more than a Pint of Juice; in the Neck of the Bottle, a little of the best Oil of Olives is to be poured, and the Cork well sealed over.

I cannot dismiss this Subject of preserving Fruits, and their Juices, at Sea, without taking Notice, that, by repeated Experiments, I find it very easy to preserve Greens, Potherbs, and proper Vegetables, a sufficient Time at Sea. The Method, however simple, is effectual; and although it may be deemed inconvenient to carry out a sufficient Quantity for the daily Use of the whole Ship's Company, yet particular Messes may reap great Advantage from it.

All have it in their Power to enjoy the green and fresh Productions of Nature; and surely Men, the most regardless of their own Health, must esteem a Dish of Greens with their salt Meat as a Delicacy, after having been some Months at Sea. The last Experiment I made, was this: On the 5th of *March*, I took a Parcel of Common Coleworts and Leeks, and, after washing them clean, shook the Water well off, and cut the Leeks into Pieces of an Inch

Inch or two in Length, and stripped the Coleworts from off the thick Stalks; then having procured two wooden Dishes, well seasoned with a strong boiled Pickle of Salt, I sprinkled, when dry, a thin Layer of pounded Bay-salt on the Bottom of each, upon which was spread a thin Layer of the Vegetable, covered with dry Bay-salt, and so alternately, until the one was filled with Coleworts, and the other with Leeks. A Cloth, wrung out of boiled salt Pickle, was afterwards put upon the Mouth of the Vessel, and the whole pressed down with a Weight. On the 5th of *June*, after they had been kept three Months, I took out a little of each, and observed the Leeks to retain their strong peculiar Flavour. After opening the Folds of the Leeks, in order to wash out the Salt, the Vegetables were put, for about ten Minutes, into cold Water to freshen, then to be boiled; when, upon a Comparison, both of them were found, in every Respect, equal to what had that Morning been taken out of the Garden. The entire Verdure and Tenderness of the Coleworts, and the perfect Flavour of the Leeks, were preserved, without the least Degree of any saline Impression.

At this Time of writing, the 5th of *January*, Greens, having been kept for ten Months, still retain, when prepared as above, for boiling, their perfect Verdure, Succulency, and Taste. It is needful to add this Caution, that earthen Vessels are improper for preserving Greens in this Manner, because the Salt in a short Time will penetrate their Substance, and the Outside of the Vessel become crusted over with saline Efflorescencies.

Further, I have with Garden Cresses Seeds, which had even been kept for two Years, raised a Salad in the Middle of Winter, in a Room where there was no Vegetation abroad: and the same is practicable in all Parts of a Ship. Let wet Cotton be spread thin on the Surface of Water, about two or three Inches from the Bottom of the Vessel, to give room for the Roots to shoot down. The Seeds being sown upon the Cotton, the Cresses will in a few Days come up.

The Water here used is not lost, it becomes strongly impregnated, both with the Flavour and Taste of Cresses; and is converted into a powerful Antidote against the Scurvy.

It is beautiful, in a Glass Vessel, to behold the daily quick Progress of Vegetation, both above and below the Surface of the Cotton.

When there is a Plenty of Water on board, or in a rainy Season, all the old Blankets may then

then be converted into Gardens; and the whole Ship both above and below, as also her Sides, be replete with Verdure. Nothing more, as I find by Experiments, being requisite, than watering the Blanket on which the Seeds are sown, twice a Day in this Climate, and allowing two Inches Room for the Roots to shoot.

But to return from a Digression, which I hope will not be deemed useless. For want of the aforementioned Fruits, or their Juices, or Shrub, I would suggest another vegetable Acid for the Use of the Navy, which is the Cream of Tartar. A Dram, or the eighth Part of an Ounce of this, will be sufficient for each Man a Day, and for half a Pint of Spirits, mixed with a Pint and a Half of Water. This Cream of Tartar is the vegetable essential Salt of Wine, and is an agreeable Acid. If the Officers, and others in the Ship, who make Use of Lemons or Oranges, would reserve the Peels to be put into the Spirits served to the Men, it would greatly improve the Flavour of the Punch, and make it little inferior to what is made with Lemon-Juice. I must add, that this is so innocent an Acid, that it may be taken in the Quantity of an Ounce or two, without producing almost

most any sensible Effect, except gently moving the Body.

It has hitherto been the Aim of those, who have made Marine Diseases their Study, to find out a proper agreeable Acid, which Sailors might be induced to use, as the best Preservative against many of their Diseases, which have been supposed to be mostly of a putrid Nature. Vinegar, Spirit of Salt, Elixir of Vitriol, and many others, have been severally recommended, and have been experienced, under proper Circumstances, to have produced good Effects: Cream of Tartar has the Advantage not only of being much more palatable than any of these Acids, and, according to the Sentiments of Doctor *Boerhaave*, and my own Experience, beneficial, and well adapted to the Constitution of Mariners; but is also the cheapest Acid that can be recommended for the Purpose. An Allowance of the eighth Part of an Ounce a Day, will not cost the Government one Shilling yearly, for each Man in the *West Indies*. I imagine the best Method is to pour a Quantity of boiling Water over-night on the Cream of Tartar, and next Morning a pure transparent Liquor, pleasantly acidulated, may be poured off from the Tartar at the Bottom. Bad Water is even thus corrected and purified. About two Pounds and a Half of the

Cream,

Cream, I think, will be sufficient to acidulate a Hogshead of Water: Or, as it is now a general Practice to mix Water with the Spirits, before serving them to the Men, a due Proportion of this Acid may be issued to each Mess, it being certain, that there are but few who would not prefer the Use of such an agreeable Acid, to Water and Rum only: And each Man having it in his Power to exchange Part of his salt Provisions (which are so detrimental to Health in hot Countries) with the Purser for Sugar, may then be daily supplied with a Quart of excellent Punch: Nay, even an Increase of the ordinary Allowance of Punch, provided it is served out at different Times of the Day, may safely be indulged, in *lieu* of the baneful salted Meats; the inflammatory Quality of the Spirit being greatly corrected by mixing it in this Manner. Hence, the Whole becomes a salutary Composition of a cooling, corroborative, antiputrid, and diuretic Nature.

The opposing Quality of Acids to the intoxicating Power of Spirits, is observable on more Occasions, than that of the Analysis of Wines. From a Mixture of Vinegar and Alcohol, will result such a Combination, as shall efface the different Tastes of the *Menstrua* in their separate State; or, in other Words, obliterate, in a manner, those Properties by
which

which they are usually distinguished. The high ardent Nature of the one becomes thus qualified and attempered by the other. And hence, whilst we are upon the Subject of potable Spirits, one Piece of Advice may not be unacceptable, in an unpitied, but somtimes dangerous Condition: I mean, the voluntary Disease of Drunkenness; a State from which Numbers never wake, and many but return to Memory, to fall the Victims of the Fever it produces: A Caution therefore may be the more needful, as it is a Case too frequent on Ship-board, and as I do not remember that its Treatment has been often spoke of.

In the Fit of Stupefaction, it is but too usual for the Delinquent to lie in an horizontal, or, what is much worse, an head-depending Position. This Situation should be immediately altered to an erect, or gently-inclined sitting Posture. If in a Bed, or Hammock, his Head should be raised, and a due Care taken that his senseless State does not change it. Warm Water, well acidulated with Mineral Acid, or Vinegar, or the Juice of Fruits, should be given him, and a Spunge dipt in Vinegar, applied to his Head, Mouth and Nose. Instances of the good Effects of this Method have been frequently experienced.

The

The Necessity there may be sometimes for blood-letting in this Case, is almost too obvious to inculcate, as well as an Emetic of gentle, but speedy Operation; Immersion of the Feet in warm Water, solutive Clysters, or whatever else may abate Distention, or take off from the Pressure above: These, I say, with plentiful Perspiration, (generally a salutary, but now a most needful Evacuation) are the usual Methods when any Extremity threatens. Those who can walk in the Air, or sit up with an over Dose of Liquor, will do well to embrace that Security, till the Kidneys, or some other Strainer, has abated the Surcharge; for going suddenly to sleep in an inebriated State, has, by Suffocation, or Apoplexy, put a Period to many Lives. This Vice of Drunkenness, one of the most destructive to our brave Seamen, ought to be discouraged by all possible Means, and severely punished by the Officers.

But let us turn our Eyes to those in a State more justly demanding the Attention of Humanity; such as have been unfortunately drowned. So soon as a Person supposed to be drowned is taken out of the Water, he ought not, as usual, to be held up long by the Heels; the Continuance in such a Posture is the most likely Means to prevent him from coming to Life. The Head must be inclined in a Position

tion favourable to empty the Stomach; mean while the utmoſt Diſpatch is uſed to remove all the cold, wet Cloaths, by ſtripping the Perſon quite naked, and immediately expoſing the Body to the Heat of the warm Sun, or a Fire, to prevent Stiffneſs and Cold; or, to regenerate Heat, he may be put in a Bed well warmed, where the Belly, Breaſt, and eſpecially the Pit of the Stomach, muſt be well and conſtantly rubbed with warm Clothes, keeping the Head and Face gently inclined forwards, as in a Perſon under the Operation of an Emetic. At the ſame time, the Limbs muſt be well chafed with hard coarſe Clothes, made very warm, and the whole Body often ſhook or rolled about. All poſſible Attempts muſt be made from the Beginning to bleed; and theſe in different Veins. The temporal Artery may alſo be cut. Warm Bricks, Irons, or Bottles of Hot Water muſt be applied to the Feet; volatile Salts, and ſtimulating Spirits to the Noſtrils; and Air, moderately heated by being near the Fire, blown by means of a Bellows into the Anus and Lungs. Or, a Perſon that chews Garlick may endeavour to blow into the Lungs with his Breath, keeping the Noſtrils of the Patient ſhut for a few Seconds of Time, to prevent its Eſcape: mean while, another Perſon, by a gentle alternate Preſſure and Dilatation of the Ribs, with a correſponding alternate Compreſſion of the Contents of the Belly upwards, imitates as near as poſſible the Act of Reſpiration in a living Body. A Clyſter of Tobacco Smoke may alſo be given, and Tobacco moiſtened, or its Juice, may be put into the Mouth, from the Stimulus of which in the Throat and Stomach, a Recovery and Vomiting has ſometimes enſued. Though theſe Means ſhould not ſpeedily produce the deſired Effect, yet the Perſon is not to be relinquiſhed. They muſt be repeated and continued for ſome Hours, keeping the Body all the while warm, or in a hot Place, perſevering in the Concuſſions and Rollings; and laſtly, he may be immerſed and kept for ſome Time in a Bath of luke-warm Water, after which, the former Means are to be again eſſayed.

When a Perſon is ſuffocated by the noxious Vapour of a Ship's Well, (an Accident not uncommon) the ſame Means are to be uſed for his Recovery, as have been preſcribed for People drowned; only there is here no Occaſion to ſtrip him of his Cloaths, till other Methods have been practiſed, eſpecially opening the Veins, &c.

And a like Method may be practiſed with thoſe ſtruck with Lightning. Accidents from Lightning are frequent on Ship-board, often

often owing to the Height of the Mafts, from which it is thrown upon the Deck. Perhaps future Experience may evince the Utility of having proper Conductors fixed at the Maft-head, or in the Shrouds; by which the Shock may be carried off from the Ship into the Sea.—Mean while, it is advifeable for the Prefervation of the Men who are expofed to it upon Deck, that, during violent Thunder and Lightning, the Officer takes the firft Opportunity of a heavy Rain falling, to employ them in fome Ship-duty, with a View that their Cloaths may become wet.

If this cannot be complied with, let fome Artifice be fallen upon, that at leaft the Hats of all the Men in the Watch be dipped in Water. This may be effected in way of Play, or Diverfion, among the People, without their knowing the Reafon of it.

As to the Officers of the Watch, they may wear a waxed Cap or Oil-Cloth, as it is called, on their Heads;—and all fhould avoid ftanding too clofe to the Foot of the Maft, or to the wet Shrouds or Ropes coming from thence.

The Principles upon which thofe Advices are founded, are too well known to require my dwelling longer on this Subject.

I fhould be wanting in my Duty to the Public, if I fhould omit, in thefe general Directions for the Prefervation of Seamen, the Ufe of Doctor *Hales*'s Ventilators*, the moft beneficial Invention for Mariners, which this Age has produced. I muft add, that the more the Men are kept in Exercife and Action during fine and calm Weather, the better will their Health be preferved: And it is each Man's Intereft to take care, that his Cheft, Cloaths, and Bedding, be often aired, and kept as free as may be from Damp and Rottennefs. Thofe, who are remifs in thefe Articles, fhould be compelled to become more cleanly.

The ordering as many of the Men as can be prevailed upon to ufe the cold Bath, either in Tubs under the Fore-caftle, or to dip in the Sea, early in the Morning, has been found extremely beneficial in warm Weather, and in hot Countries. The Body is thereby cooled and refrefhed, the Fibres braced and invigorated, fo that the Men become afterwards better enabled to undergo the Fatigues and Heat of the Day. This would prove not

---

* See his Book on Ventilators.

only

only an excellent Means of Health, but of Cleanliness: And indeed it has been found experimentally true, that the cold Bath is of sovereign Use to the *Europeans* in the Torrid Zone; and that by cleansing the Skin, and invigorating the whole Habit, it is so far from stopping the plentiful and necessary cuticular Discharges in hot Weather, that it promotes them. I can affirm, from my own Experience in hot Climates, that many Diarrhœas, and other Complaints, the pure and sole Effect of an unusual and great Heat, (relaxing the System of the Solids, and occasioning a Colliquation of the animal Juices) have not only been cured by Cold Bathing, but the Return, and even the Attack, of such Diseases, effectually prevented by it.

I am persuaded that the remarkable Healthfulness of the *Tyger* Ship of War, commanded by Captain *Latham*, in her late Voyage to the *East-Indies*, was more owing to the Use of the Cold Bath, than to any other Circumstance regarding the Ship, or her Company*. It is indeed worthy of Observation,

---

* See a Letter from Captain *Latham*, inserted in the *Gentleman's Magazine*, in the Month of *April*, 1755. It is dated from St. *Augustin's Bay*, in the Island of *Madegascar*, 9th of *September*, 1754.

that, in this Voyage, two Ships kept together in Company, and were pretty much of the same Rate; yet, at the End of the Run, one of them had above two hundred Men sick on board, whilst the other had not above nine or ten. This proves, I think to a Demonstration, that very minute Circumstances in a Ship often occasion, or prevent, a general Sickness, and consequently a great Mortality in a Voyage.

Most People know, that the Cold Bath, though very serviceable in sultry Weather, and at such a Time often absolutely necessary, as I have experienced in my own Person in hot Countries, yet may be injudiciously and preposterously used. The Abuses are too long Duration in the Water, or when the Sailors are permitted to go into it over-heated with Work or Liquor, when the Stomach is full, or when a critical Eruption, called the prickly Heat, appears upon the Skin.

These general Directions being premised, I proceed to treat more particularly of such Diseases as are usual, or may be apprehended, in hot, sultry, and unwholesome Climates; with a View to point out what promises the most certain Protection against their Attacks.

The

The firſt Diſtempers which generally occur in a Voyage to the Southward, are, for the moſt part, of an inflammatory Nature, and owing to a ſudden Tranſition from cold to hot Weather. This occaſions a Fulneſs and Diſtention of the Veſſels; hence, ſuch Diſorders, and hence, all *Europeans*, upon their firſt Arrival under the Tropic, bear Evacuations much better than afterwards. It has been a common Practice at Sea, to bleed a Number of the Ship's Company, when firſt they come into a warm Latitude, by way of Prevention: But Experience does not ſhew, that this Operation has any ſuch Effect upon their future Health; nor can the Propriety of bleeding almoſt all the Men, as it is often done in the Merchant's Service, without Diſtinction of Age, Conſtitution, *&c.* be well juſtified; though we allow Bleeding, in ſome particular Caſes, uſeful at this Time, and neceſſary. I ſhall endeavour elſewhere * to particularise the Caſes in which this Operation is needful; let it ſuffice for the preſent to obſerve, that previous Blood-letting is not to be depended upon as a Security againſt the Diſeaſes of intemperate Climates.

* In the Appendix.

It often, indeed, happens, that the Men enjoy an uninterrupted State of Health in the Torrid Zone, when the Ship meets with fine favourable Weather, and has a good Paſſage, and eſpecially when ſhe leaves *England* in the Autumn, and arrives at *Jamaica*, or other Places to the northward of the Æquator, when the Sun is pretty well advanced towards the ſouthern Tropic: It being generally upon their Arrival in Harbour, and after anchoring in ſickly Places, that the Men are attacked with the Diſeaſes of the Country.

The contrary, however, may happen, and it has been remarked, that when Ships crouded with Men* have a tedious Paſſage, or are long becalmed at Sea, during a Continuance of hot, moiſt, and cloſe Weather; or when they ſuffer by heavy Rains, uſual in their Seaſon, within the Tropics, Diſeaſes different from

---

* It is a Miſtake deſtructive to the Men to croud too many of them together in a Southern Voyage, or in a hot Climate, as the Ship will be found, before the End of the Voyage, in much more Diſtreſs for want of Men, than ſhe would have been, had ſhe at firſt carried out only her proper Complement. An additional Number is often made, in order to ſupply an expected Mortality; but they generally encreaſe that Mortality to double or triple their own Number. This Fact has been often confirmed by Experience in foreign Services, and lately in the *Pitt*, an *Eaſt-India* armed Ship, and ſeveral others.

the

the former, and much more fatal to the Men than thofe of the inflammatory Kind, begin to appear.

A few of the Sailors are fometimes at firſt ſeized with Fluxes, which denote a Difpoſition in the Air to Putrefaction, and to beget a malignant Fever of the remitting, or intermitting Form, moſt frequently of the double tertian Kind. This Fever, which is the genuine Produce of Heat and Moiſture, is the Epidemic between the Tropics, upon the Coaſt of *Guinea*, and in *Jamaica*; and is the autumnal Fever of all hot Countries: It is extremely different from what is called the yellow Fever, or black Vomit, which is rare, and takes place only among a Few, on their firſt Arrival in the *Weſt-Indies*[*]. In large Ships and

---

[*] Since the firſt Edition was printed, I tranfmitted ſome Queries relating to the Difeafes in the *Weſt-Indies*, to Mr. *Naſmyth*, an ingenious Gentleman, and Surgeon to Admiral *Holmes* at *Jamaica*, and received the following Anſwers from *Port-Royal*, dated *April* 15, 1761.

" *Q.* Is not the common Fever of *Jamaica* of the
" remitting Kind, and nearly ſuch as has been deſcribed
" by *Cleghorn*, as the Epidemic of *Minorca?*

" *A.* The Remitting Fever is truly one of the fixed
" regular Epidemics of this Iſland; and is more or leſs
" prevalent

and Fleets, it would seem to be generated among the Sailors by Contagion, by their great

" prevalent in the Months of *October*, *November*, and
" *December*. I look upon it to be the same as that of *Mi-*
" *norca*, of *Sumatra*, of *Java*, and of many other Places
" in the *East* and *West-Indies*, between the Tropics.
" Here, from the great Extent of Country, large Tracts
" of uncultivated Land, Woods, Marshes, and a consi-
" derable Degree of Heat and Moisture; from these, I
" say, and other Causes, this Fever is found to act with
" full Vigour, and often proves very fatal. It terminates
" sometimes as common Fevers do, by the Skin, Kid-
" neys, or Intestines; though oftner, and with more
" Safety, as a regular Intermittent; when it is readily
" subdued by the Bark, &c.

" *Q.* Wherein does it differ from the Yellow Fever?

" *A.* An Inflammatory *Diathesis*, with dense Blood dis-
" posing to Obstruction, very commonly introduces *the Re-*
" *mitting Fever*: The Heat too, except in the Remission,
" is pretty equal; and seldom any Signs of Dissolution in
" the Blood, or Tendency to Putrefaction, appear, until
" the Disease has has been of some Standing.——*The*
" *Yellow Fever*, in at least ninety Patients of a hundred,
" exhibits immediate Appearances of Colliquation and
" approaching Putrefaction. The Blood, in the Begin-
" ning, is commonly loose and dissolved: The great Heat
" soon subsides, when a clammy Moisture succeeds. In
" this State the Heat is really under the Standard of
" Health; and then it is that Putrefaction becomes general
" and active.

" *Q.*

great Intemperance, and conſtant Uſe of a groſs, corrupted, ſalt Diet, altogether unſuitable to the Climate.

But

" *Q.* Are the Patients in this laſt Fever ſubject to profuſe
" Hæmorrhages, or other Symptoms of remarkable Colli-
" quation or Putrefaction of the Blood?

" *A.* From the early and general Diſſolution of the
" Blood, Hæmorrhages are very frequent in this laſt Fe-
" ver; and theſe too from almoſt every Part of the Body:
" The Gums, the Noſe, the Corners of the Eyes, give
" early Proofs of this. Sometimes bloody Exudations
" from the Fore-head, the Arm-pits, from cicatrized
" Wounds, large black Spots, and fœtid cadaverous Ex-
" cretions of every Kind, confirm the general State of
" Putrefaction.

" *Q.* What Diſeaſes do you imagine are produced at
" Sea, by the great Heat in the *Weſt-Indies*, where Infec-
" tion and the Land Exhalation can be ſuppoſed to have
" no Influence?

" *A.* I have remarked in the Courſe of ſome Voyages
" to the *Eaſt-Indies*, (theſe, you know, afford the faireſt
" Trials) that the Inconveniencies and Diſeaſes ariſing
" from *mere Heat*, are far leſs conſiderable than is com-
" monly imagined. The immediate and moſt frequent
" Effect of hot Air, is Rarefaction of the Fluids, hence
" different Degrees of Fever, from the accelerated Pulſe,
" ſlight Head-ach, &c. to a Phrenſy and highly ardent
" Fever.

" Upon

But to return to the true Epidemic in the Torrid Zone; I have found, by manifold Experience, in the moſt unhealthy Rivers upon the Coaſt of *Guinea*, that the Safety of the Patient, in this Diſeaſe, entirely depended upon the Fever's intermitting; or at leaſt, its remitting ſo favourably, as might affordan Opportunity of throwing in half an Ounce, or an Ounce, of the Jeſuits Bark. The Bark is indeed, at this Time, univerſally known, by Practitioners of all Nations, to be the only ſovereign Medicine for this moſt frequent and malignant Fever, in thoſe ſickly ſouthern Climates.

In the Courſe of my Inquiries into this Subject, I have had an Opportunity of conſulting the Journals, kept in thoſe Voyages

"Upon the Subject of Thermometers, about which
"you ſeem to be inquiſitive; I muſt tell you, that I have
"generally been provided with ſeveral; and, in this pre-
"ſent Voyage, have endeavoured, as much as poſſible, to
"diſcover the Influence of Heat in the Production and
"Courſe of Diſeaſes;—for this Purpoſe, I aſcertained,
"with great Exactneſs, the Number of Men lodged upon
"each Deck; where lodged when taken ill, and of what
"Diſtemper. My Obſervations of the Mercury were
"at proper ſtated Times, and attended with general Re-
"marks of the Weather; notwithſtanding this Exactneſs
"and Attention, I cannot at this preſent Time ſettle any
"thing ſatisfactory or worthy of your Notice."

by

by many ingenious Surgeons of Ships of War; and, however irregular, or diverſified under different Appearances, this Fever might ſhew itſelf, I found the Diſtemper was eſſentially the ſame, and that the Bark alone, judiciouſly adminiſtered during a Remiſſion, or Intermiſſion, proved the moſt certain Means of Cure. Many Inſtances might be produced, ſeveral Hiſtories of Fevers might here be related, wherein the Efficacy of the Bark would be fully evinced. I ſhall only obſerve, that the Fever of the Iſland of *St. Thomas*, is, to a Proverb in that Part of the World, deemed the moſt malignant and fatal Species of any *African* or *American* Fever: But by a very accurate Account of this Fever, which I have had Occaſion to peruſe, it would appear, that the Bark is likewiſe the beſt Remedy.

It is again to be obſerved, that this Remedy proves not only a Specific for this univerſal malignant, remitting, or intermitting Fever, but the continued Uſe of it is an effectual Preſervative againſt a Relapſe. Hence one would naturally infer, that the Uſe of the Bark would prevent the Attack of this Sickneſs; and, accordingly, Experience (the ſureſt Guide and Standard of Medical Truths) teſtifies, that the Bark proves a Defence againſt the Attack of this Fever, and other

malignant

malignant Diforders, which may be apprehended in unfalutary Climates, and during a corrupt and malignant Difpofition of the Air.

——This Hint, I firft received when on the Coaft of *Guinea*. I was informed, that the Factories were furnifhed with proper Quantities of the *Cortex*, by the late *African* Company, which was taken by way of Prevention, during the rainy and fickly Seafon; and that it was attended with remarkable Succefs in fuch as could be brought to fubmit to a regular Courfe of Life, and to refrain from eating fuch Quantities of animal Food as they were wont to do in *England*, which yearly deftroys many on that Coaft. I have fince been confirmed in my Opinion, of the Succefs to be expected from the Ufe of the Bark, taken by way of Prefervative, by many Confiderations and Facts: I fhall produce only one of the latter.

Hungary is acknowledged to be the moft fickly Climate in *Europe*, and indeed, as bad as any in the World. Here it was, where the Chriftian Armies, in marching only through the Country, in the Expeditions againft the *Saracens*, formerly called the *Croifadoes*, often loft half of their Number, from the fickly Quality of the Country; and where the *Auftrians*, not long fince, buried, in a few Years, above

above 40,000 of their beſt Troops, who fell a Sacrifice to the malignant Diſpoſition of the *Hungarian* Air.—— Now the ſame Cauſes, which ſubſiſt in an eminent Degree in *Hungary*, render ſome ſouthern Countries injurious to the Health and Conſtitution of Strangers. *Hungary* abounds in Rivers, which, by often overflowing, leave that low, flat Country, overſpread with Lakes and Ponds of ſtagnating Water, and with large, unwholſome, putrifying Marſhes. So great is the Impurity of theſe ſtagnant Waters, that by them the Rivers, even the *Danube*, whoſe Courſe is ſlow, becomes, in Places, tainted and ſtinking.

The Air is moiſt, and, in Summer, quite ſultry. In the Nights of Harveſt, it was ſo very damp, that we are told *, the *Auſtrian* Soldiers could not ſhelter themſelves from the Moiſture by a triple Tent-Covering.

Epidemical Diſtempers begin conſtantly to rage in the hotteſt Months, which are *July*, *Auguſt*, and *September*. Theſe Complaints, according to the accurate Obſervations of a

* Vide *Krameri* Obſervationes de Climate *Hungarico*.

Phyſician,

Physician *, who practised long in *Hungary*, are altogether the same with those which are epidemic upon the Coast of *Guinea*, and in the sickly Climates of the *East* and *West Indies*, viz. malignant, remitting, and intermitting Fevers, Dysenteries, and Diarrhœas.

The Heat of the Sun in Summer is more intense in *Hungary* (according to my Author) than in any other Part of *Europe*, and, in Proportion to the Heat, the more pestiferous are the marshy Exhalations. It is constantly observed, that the nearer any City or Fort is situated to a Morass, or an ample River, with foul and oozy Banks, the more unhealthy the Inhabitants. At such Seasons, and Places, the Air swarms with numberless Insects and Animalcules, a sure Sign of its putrid and malignant Disposition.

The hotter the Summer, the more frequent and mortal the Diseases. This was fatally experienced by the *Austrians*, in the unusual sultry Summer-Months of the Year 1717, and 1718, when they found the Climate of *Hungary* a much more dreadful and destructive Enemy, than the assailing *Turks*.

* Doctor *Kramer*, Physician to the Imperial Army.

In the former of these Years, at the Siege of *Belgrade*, the Fever of the Country, and the Dysentery, occasioned a very singular and extraordinary Mortality among the Troops. The Dread of these Diseases caused every one (as may naturally be supposed) to have Recourse to different Precautions for Self-preservation. The great Prince *Eugene*, who commanded in Chief, had Water, and the Provisions for his Table, sent him twice a Week from *Vienna*. The pure Stream of the River *Kahlenberg* was regularly brought to him: He avoided all Excesses, and lived regularly, or rather abstemiously; refreshed himself often by eating a cool Melon, and mixed his usual Wine, which was *Burgundy*, with Water. But, notwithstanding his utmost Care, this illustrious Hero was seized with a dangerous Dysentery, which would have quickly terminated Life, had not the speedy Conclusion of that Campaign, permitted him a quick Retreat.*

At

---

* From what *Kramer* and others have advanced, concerning the pernicious Constitution of the *Hungarian* Air, we may account for the vast, and almost uniform Fatality of the variolous, and other pestilential Diseases, to which that Country is unhappily subject. A living Author (*Weszpremi*, de Inoculanda Peste, 1754) a Native of *Tockay*, observes, that their extended Deserts and desolated Cities witness the dreadful Devastations made by

the

At this unhealthy Season, when hardly one Imperial Officer, much less their several Domestics, escaped those malignant Sicknesses, the renowned Count *Bonneval*, and his numerous Retinue, continued, amidst this pestilential Contagion, in perfect Health, to the Surprize, or, to use my Author's Words, the Envy of all who beheld him. The only Precaution he used, was to take, two or three Times a Day, a small Quantity of Brandy, in which the Bark was infused; and he obliged all his Attendants and Domestics to follow his Example.

It is no less remarkable, that the *Count*, placing his certain Preservation in the Use of this simple Bitter, lived for many Years afterwards in the most unhealthy Spots of *Hungary*, without any Attack, or Apprehension of Disease; and continued to enjoy a perfect State of Health, during the hottest and most sickly Seasons. And thus, with an unbroken and sound Constitution, which is seldom the Case of those who reside long in such Climates, he lived to a great Age.

the malignant Evils of this Soil. A Province, says he, which requires great and annual Supplies of Colonies from fruitful *Swabia*, to reinstate those whom Disease has sacrificed.

There

There is an Instance produced by the same Author,* of a whole Regiment in *Italy* having been preserved, by the Use of the Bark, from the Attack of the same malignant Diseases, *viz.* the Dysentery and Bilious Fever (as it is often called) when the rest of the *Austrian* Army, not pursuing that Method, became greatly annoyed.

But from what has been already said, there is Reason to presume, I think with a great Degree of Certainty, that, if his Majesty's Ships, when bound on a Voyage to any of the afore-mentioned unhealthy Climates, were supplied with a due Quantity of the Bark, it might prove effectual for preventing both the Bilious Fever, and Bloody Flux, the latter being the same Disease falling upon the Intestines.

This might be made extremely palatable, by infusing it in Spirits, especially if a little Orange-Peel be added. The Orange-Flavour renders it a Bitter of an agreeable Taste, and conceals what is offensive in the Bark. Eight Ounces of Bark, and four Ounces of dried Orange-Peel, infused in a Gallon of

---

* Dr. *Kramer.*

Spirits,* will make a much more agreeable bitter Dram, than what the Sailors often make up for themselves at Sea, of Gentian, Snake-root, and other disagreeable aromatic Ingredients.———Two Ounces of this Composition, which will be but a very moderate Dram to a Sailor, may be allowed to each Man a Day, upon the Approach or Apprehension of these malignant Diseases.

It, indeed, would be still better, if the Men were to be served with only Half of this Quantity, to be taken upon an empty Stomach in the Morning, and the other Half, when they are called out to their Night-Watch.

It does not appear, to me, necessary to subjoin any Cautions † in the Use of so excellent

and

---

* The Spirit may be impregnated with a much greater Quantity of Bark, if needful, for a more effectual Preservation. To which I know no other Objection than that the Taste will not be so agreeable. Spirits will extract the Virtues of a triple Quantity of Bark here proposed, and thence will become much more efficacious. It is usual now in some of the *Guinea* Factories, when taking the Bark, to keep the Body gently lax by a Draught of Sea Water occasionally taken in a Morning. Those who dislike Spirits, may use the Bark infused in Wine, or boiled in Water.

† Where there is Apprehension of Sickness, the best Precepts are those delivered by *Celsus*, viz. To avoid

too

and harmless a stomachic Bitter, taken in so small a Quantity as is here directed. A whole Ounce of Bark has been swallowed, in less than two Hours, upon an empty Stomach, by Persons in Health, without their being able to perceive from it the least sensible, much less any bad Effect.* Its long continued Use is observed neither to offend the weakest hysteric Female-Constitution, nor to ruffle the most sensible and feeble System of Nerves and Solids in Men.

It may seem deviating from the Plan proposed in this short Essay, which is to state Facts, and not to frame Hypotheses, to offer any theoretic Opinions concerning the Manner, by which this *Indian* Drug produces so singular and salutary Effects. However, I

too great Fatigue, Indigestions, or Crudities in the Stomach, immoderate Cold as well as great Heat, and Excesses of every Kind: More especially, at such a Season, the Constitution is not to be weakened by Bleeding and Purging, for the Sake of Prevention. If at this Time the Stomach, or Intestines, are oppressed with Crudities, or sharp bilious Humours, these may be gently carried off by a Draught of Salt-water, or by a mild Laxative of Rhubarb, or rather by a gentle Emetic, shunning all great Evacuations of the Body as hurtful.

* Vid. Dissert. Medic. de *Cortice Peruviano*, p. 14. Auctore, Cheney Hart.

cannot

cannot help obferving, that, by what we difcover of this Bark by our Senfes and Experience, it is an agreeable aromatic Aftringent, and one of the beft ftomachic Bitters. Hence, being endued with fuch Qualities, it muft needs, like all other Bitters, ftrengthen the Stomach, and promote the Digeftion of fuch hard and tenacious Food, as the *Englifh* Sailors live upon at Sea; and it further prevents the Generation of that grofs and vifcid Chyle, which is the confequent Production of that Food. Such are certainly good Purpofes, which it may anfwer, but the more important are thefe: It braces the relaxed Fibres of the Body, (a relaxed Habit being the conftant Effect of Heat and Moifture) and, at the fame time, by keeping up a free Perfpiration, and by maintaining a conftant and equable Circulation of the Blood, and other Juices, it effectually prevents their Tendency to a Lentor, Stagnation, and Putrefaction.

Thefe are well known to Phyficians to be the immediate Caufes, in the human Body, of the fatal intermitting, and of the putrid Diftempers in hot and unwholfome Climates. We have indeed the moft ample Experience of the Efficacy of this Remedy, in refifting and ftopping Putrefaction. In the Small-pox, when there is a gangrenous Difpofition, and in many other external Mortifications,

Mortifications, even when that deadly Procefs is far advanced, this Remedy gives fo powerful and fudden a Check, that it appears to be the ftrongeft Antifeptic, taken inwardly, of any yet difcovered: It is, indeed, peculiarly fuitable to the Conftitution in hot Climates,* as alfo to their endemic Difeafes; and thefe, its divine Virtues, were known to the Native *Indians*, long before our Arrival among them.

But to proceed. As the Weather, remote from Land in the Torrid *Zone*, is, for the greateft Part of the Year, dry and ferene, the exceffive Heat being much moderated by a conftant, refrefhing, and uniform Breeze, the Men often enjoy a better State of Health at Sea, than when they arrive in Harbour, or get within Reach of the noxious Vapours, which arife from many Parts of the Land.

The particular unhealthy Seafons of the Year, the Harbours and Coafts moft fatal to *Europeans*, are now generally known. Such Places, Prudence directs to be avoided; but this Expedient for Health cannot always be complied with. Neceffity often obliges Ships to put into Parts, where Sicknefs may be juftly apprehended; in order to guard againft

---

* See the Appendix.

which, as much as the Situation of Things will permit, they ought to be furnished with some other necessary Directions.

It may, in general, be remarked, that, in sultry Climates, or during hot Weather, in all Places subject to great Rains, where the Country is not cleared and cultivated, but is over-run with Thickets, Shrubs, or Woods, especially if there are Marshes, *Lagunes*, or stagnating Waters in the Neighbourhood, Sickness may be dreaded, and such a malignant Fever of the remitting or intermitting Kind, as has been often mentioned. The Fens, even in different Counties of *England*, are known to be very dangerous to the Health of those who live near them, and still more so to Strangers; but the woody and marshy Lands in hot Countries are exceedingly more pernicious to the Health of *Europeans*.

When Ships are necessarily obliged to put into such unhealthy Parts, the first Precaution to be taken, is, to anchor at as great a Distance from the Shore as can well be done.— To prefer the open Sea, where the Anchorage is safe, to running up into Rivers or Bays inclosed with the Land, and especially where there are high Mountains, that may intercept the salutary Current of Sea Breezes. The

higher

higher Ships fail up the Rivers upon the Coast of *Guinea*, the more sickly they become: Such, however, as keep at Sea, beyond the Reach of the Land Breeze*, are, for the most part, healthy.

It is not to be expected, that we should be able precisely to determine the Distance, to which the Sphere of unhealthy Vapours, from such woody swampy Ground, does extend itself; as this must, at all Times, greatly depend upon the blowing of the Wind from that Quarter. Thus, at *Rome*, the South-East Wind, termed, by the *Italians*, *Scirocco*, which passes over the adjacent Marshes, is most unsalutary; and yet the Effects of this Wind have been experienced to extend only to those Parts of the City, which lay nearest them, occasioning an epidemic Fever, whilst the rest of the City was free †.

That the Malignity of Air, which we are now relating, does often not extend it Influence to any considerable Distance, is farther proved by manifold Experience. " In " the Year 1747, when some of the *British* " Troops, partly in Camp and Cantonments

---

* Two or three Leagues at Sea.

† Lancis. de nox. palud. Effluv. Lib ii. Epid. i. Cap. 3.

" in Zealand, suffered an excessive Sickness
" from the marshy bad Air, insomuch that
" not a seventh Part of the Corps, stationed
" there, was fit for Duty; Commodore
" *Mitchel*'s Squadron, which lay at that Time
" at Anchor, in the Channel, between *South*
" *Beveland*, and the Island of *Walcheren*, in
" both which Places the Distemper raged,
" was neither afflicted with Fever nor Flux,
" but, amidst all that Sickness, enjoyed per-
" fect Health." A Proof, says the learned
Author [*], that the moist and putrid Air of
the Marshes was dissipated, or corrected, before it could reach them.

How far soever the noxious Vapours, from
unhealthy Grounds, may spread themselves,
it is demonstrable, that their Malignity de-
creases in Proportion to the Distance to which
they are diffused. Thus, when Commodore
Long's Squadron, in the Months of *July* and
August, 1744, lay off the Mouth of the *Tiber*,
I observed one or two of the Ships, which
lay closest to the Shore, began to be affected
by the pernicious Vapour from the Land;
whilst some others, lying farther out at Sea,
at but a very small Distance from the former,
had not a Man sick. At the same Time, the
Austrian Army, under the Command of Prince

---

[*] Dr. *Pringle*, in his excellent Observations on the Diseases of the Army. Part I. Chap. 7.

Lobcowitz,

Lobcowitz, suffered so great a Sickness, through the Proximity of their Situation to the marshy Country, that they were obliged to decamp.

The Facts which have been recited, will, I hope, engage due Attention to one very important Direction for preserving the Health of the Men, when a Ship puts into a Harbour, where Sickness may be apprehended from a low, marshy, uncultivated Country; which is, that the Ship be anchored in the best-aired Station, where she may be well exposed to the Sea Breezes, and, as much as possible, to the Windward of the Woods and Marshes: And the same Precautions are to be taken, when arriving at the sickly Season in those Climates; that is, either during, or soon after, a rainy Constitution of the Atmosphere.

The Success of Expeditions in the *East* or *West Indies*, greatly depends upon their being executed in the most proper Season of the Year; and the Ships, upon their Arrival before the Place, should, if possible, lie open to the Wind, as one of the best Preservatives against the Maladies of a neighbouring sickly Country; it having been often experienced, in those dangerous Climates, that riding safe from the Wind, in secure Creeks, and stifling close Havens, surrounded with interposing Mountains,

tains, has proved the Destruction of Fleets at an Anchor, while their Cruisers at Sea have enjoyed perfect Health.

If, in such Climates, it should happen, that it is impossible to avoid anchoring close to the Land, and even in a Harbour, where the Ship is quite encompassed with Woods, Mountains, and swampy Ground, to alleviate, as much as possible, this Misfortune, some other Precautions may be taken.

The first, that I shall mention, is——That the Crew be kept at Work, upon Deck, as little as the Nature of the Service will permit, before Sun-rising, or after Sun-setting, and indeed, only when the Sea Breeze blows. This Advice is founded upon an Observation, that when the Sun is above the Horizon, the noxious Land-Vapours are more dispersed; they are then much rarer than in the Night, or even in the Evenings and Mornings, when they become denser, and more apt to affect. Add to this, that the Land-Wind vigorously conveys them in a more abundant Quantity towards the Ship. Now, the Night-Air at Land, in those southern Climates, is always very moist, occasioned by the excessive Dews; and those Dews are experienced to be extremely pernicious to such Persons, as are

exposed

expofed to them*. But, although we may fuppofe the falling Dews to be impregnated with unfavourable Exhalations, from the Earth or Land-Air, it is neverthelefs certain, that extreme Moifture greatly favours the Exertion of their unfriendly Influences.

That an impure Air has an Effect, in proportion to its Moifture, upon the Health of the Men, and even upon the moft hardy Conftitutions, would appear by the following curious Experiment.

In the Year 1748, upon the breaking up of the *Britifh* Camp in *Flanders*, the Cavalry were cantoned in the unhealthy Ground about *Bois-le-duc*, and foon after were attacked with a very general Sicknefs, occafioned by the late Inundations of that Part of the Country. Dr. *Home*, then Surgeon to *Cope*'s Dra-

---

* In *Arabia*, and fome other Eaftern Countries, the *Dews* are experienced to have none of thofe bad Qualities. But in *Guinea*, and in many Parts of the *Eaft* and *Weft-Indies*, the Dews on fhore have been extremely fatal to many *Europeans*; more efpecially when, molefted with the Heat within Doors, and the Plague of Mofchitoes, they have ventured to fleep in the open Night-Air. The *Negroes* and *Creoles*, fleeping without Hurt in the Dews, is a Proof how far the Conftitution may be framed and accuftomed to bear what otherwife is fo highly prejudicial.

goons, observes *, that the Troops suffered in Proportion to their Proximity to the Marshes, and that universally, the nearer to *Bois-le-duc*, the more violent was the Distemper: The Number of the Sick, by a very accurate Observation, being found exactly to correspond with the Dampness of their Situation, and of the Air. To put this Matter beyond all Doubt, this ingenious Gentleman provided himself with a good *Hygroscope*, by which he carefully measured, every Day, the Degree of Moisture or Dryness in the Air; and, upon comparing his Tables with the Register kept of the Sick, he found, that the Progress of the Disease kept an exact Pace with the Humidity of the Air.

On the 29th of *June* they left the Camp, and from that Day to the 12th of *July*, the Air being dry, not one Soldier was affected with an Ailment. On the Evening of the 12th, the *Hygrometer* indicated a great Degree of Moisture in the Air, and that very Night the epidemic Sickness (*viz.* the remitting Fever) began among the Troops; three Dragoons of *Cope*'s Regiment being seized with it. During eight Days afterwards, the Air

† In an elegant Performance, entitled, *Dissertat. Medica inaug. de Febre remittente*, p. 14, &c.

continued

continued extremely moift, and the Number of the Sick was proportionally increafed. The ten following Days being drier, the Number of the infected vifibly diminifhed. But two very moift Days fucceeding, the Patients were again greatly encreafed. In a Word, the fame Quality of the Air, which differently affected the Inftrument, did alfo every Day, in like Manner, affect the Health of the Men. *

When a Ship at Anchor is near marfhy Ground or Swamps, efpecially during Summer or in hot Weather, and the Wind blows directly from thence, the Gun-Ports, which would admit fuch a noxious Land-Breeze, ought to be kept fhut. Or, if the Ship rides with her Head to the Wind, a thick Sail ought to be put upon the Fore-maft, along which, the Smoke from the Galley might be made conftantly to play and afcend. If the Sail fhould occafion a little falutary Smoak

---

* Though Moifture proceeding from the Earth or Ground, is truly the moft baneful, yet every Practitioner muft have perceived very fenfible Effects on the Conftitution, from a raw, moift Atmofphere, and during rainy Weather. Thus, even in this Country, the being expofed to moift eafterly Winds is very apt to produce Agues and intermitting Fevers, and efpecially to occafion Relapfes into fuch Diforders.

between Decks, this Inconvenience will be sufficiently compensated, by its keeping off the full and streight Stream of the swampy Shore-Effluvia, which now being obliged to form a Curve before they reach the more distant Parts of the Vessel, must needs be greatly diverted and scattered. At such Seasons, the Men may be enjoined to smoke Tobacco, and the Carpenters to fumigate the Ship often with the wholesome Steams of Pitch or Tar.

'Tis constantly experienced, that the greatest Sufferers in unhealthy Harbours are the Boats Crews, and such, as being employed in the necessary Business of wooding and watering the Ship, are obliged to sleep on Shore. That the Men, on these Duties, are so suddenly and universally seized with Sickness, is commonly ascribed to their Intemperance, or their being wet in the Night with Rain, from the Insufficiency of their Tents, &c. But the Truth is, their nearer Approach to the unwholesome Land-Air, and especially their sleeping in it, are the real Causes of their being infected. This is demonstrable from the Nature of the Malady which they contract, which is very different from the Effects of Drunkenness, or of a common Cold, and is constantly the peculiar endemic Disease of the Country. One great Means then of the Safety

of

of the Men, which are employed on Shore, would be to relieve them often, and to permit none to sleep in the Tents. Centinels should be placed with a Midshipman at the watering Place, and strictly charged to prohibit Sleep; for in Sleep, (a State of general Relaxation) there is the greatest Danger from the unwholesome Air. This is a Thing so well known at *Rome*, that, of its many Inhabitants, there is scarce to be found one of the better Sort, who, during Summer or Autumn, would venture to sleep a Night at *Ostia*, or in the Neighbourhood of the Marshes adjoining to the City. Persons often recreate in the Day, and hunt in the unhealthy Parts of the Campania, but they are sure to return to the City before Night; the fatal Experience of many having sufficiently taught them the Danger of sleeping in those Nurseries of Disease *.

---

* It has been an ancient received Maxim, that to rise early, was greatly conducive to Health. This, in a qualified Sense, is true. The Practice implies, Regularity the preceding Night; and, in dry and lofty Situations, the Propriety of this Adage will the best appear. But woody, marshy, and low maritime Places, with those subject to Inundations, are manifest Exceptions to the Rule. The Inhabitants of such Districts, if they would secure themselves from febrile and other consequent Attacks of their raw and uncorrected Atmosphere, should wait the Sun's Appearance

I remember in the Year 1739, when Admiral *Haddock* arrived with the Fleet under his Command in *Mahon* Harbour, a Midshipman and eight or ten Men from each Ship, were ordered to remain on Shore, with the Coopers at the Watering-Place, to refit and fill the Water-Casks. This Watering-Place was in a Creek of the Harbour, well known by the Name of *English-Cove*. Here the Men found a very large artificial Cave, dug out of a soft sandy Stone, sufficient to contain their whole Number. Their Bedding was directly carried thither, and it being in the Summer-Months, the agreeable Coolness of the Re-

Appearance in, if not his Advance above, the Horizon, before they attempt the Business of the Field. To select a domestic Instance, amidst a Variety producible on this Occasion, take that of a Clergyman of long Observation in such Matters, who has assured me, that few of the Farmers, reputed early Risers in his Parish, which is near the level Coast of *Holderness*, live to be old. Defluxions on the Breast and Lungs, Rheumatisms, Intermittents, and the Diseases of a debilitated Tone of Fibres, and slackened Perspiration, are the Evils entailed on their mistaken Conduct.

In *Europe* the Colour of the Inhabitants gives the true Indications of the Healthfulness of the Soil. Thus in most Places of the *Isle of Wight* the Natives shew in their Countenances the most visible Tokens of confirmed Health, compared with those who even inhabit the Island of *Portsea*, but especially those in the fenny Countries.

treat

treat was deemed by them all highly refreshing. But the Consequence was, every one who slept in this damp Place, became infected with the Tertian Fever, then epidemic in *Minorca*; of which not one in eight recovered. Most of the Coopers belonging to the Fleet, were at this Time cut off by it. Whilst at the same Time, the Men on board the Ships, who lay close almost to the Shore, were free from Complaint. And others, who were ordered upon the same Duty of watering the Fleet, in the Place of those who were taken ill, enjoyed likewise a perfect State of Health, by being obliged to sleep every Night in their respective Ships. There are numerous Instances of Boats Crews having suffered greatly by sleeping near the Mangroves, with which the Sides of the Rivers are frequently planted in the Torrid Zone. I have known the whole Crew seized next Morning with bad Fevers, and seen several Men at *Haslar* Hospital, whom the Fever, thus contracted, had left in a cachectic and irrecoverable bad State of Health.

As for those who must of necessity remain on Shore, and sleep in dangerous Desarts and uninhabited Places, some farther Directions should be added for their Use.—They must take Care not to sleep upon the Ground exposed to the Dews, but in Hammocks in a close

close Tent, standing upon a dry Sand, Gravel, or Chalk near the Sea-Shore, and where there is no subterraneous Water for at least four Feet below the Surface of the Ground. The Door of this Tent should be made to open towards the Sea, and the back Part of it, which receives the Land-Breeze, must be well secured by double Canvas, or covered with Branches of Trees. When the Air is thick, moist and chill, the Earth being overspread with cold Dew, a constant Fire must be kept in or near the Tent, as the most excellent Means of purifying such unwholesome Air, and of preserving the Health of those, who either sleeping or waking, are exposed to its Influence. The Centinels who guard the Water-Casks, ought likewise at such a Time to have a Fire burning near them. All old and forsaken Habitations, convenient Caves, and natural Grottos in the Earth, where the Men may be induced to take up their Abode, must, before their Admission, be perfectly dried and purified with sufficient Fires; likewise every Person should be made to observe the necessary Caution of wearing warmer Cloaths and Coverings, as a Defence from the chilling nocturnal Air.

Let all, who value their Health, also have Recourse upon these Occasions, Evening and Morning,

Morning, to a Dram of the bitter Infufion of the Bark: Or, if this cannot be procured, they may ufe a moderate Dram of Garlic-Brandy. Expofure to the too great Heat of the Sun is carefully to be avoided.

Thofe Seamen or Officers who are employed on Shore in unhealthful Countries, may be allowed to indulge themfelves in a more plentiful, tho' moderate Ufe of Vinous or Spirituous Liquors. In Ague-producing, hot, and intemperate Climates, a light Dinner, but a more hearty Supper, with a Glafs in the Evening, will not be amifs, for fuch as have been accuftomed to free living.

But Fire and Smoke being undoubtedly the great Purifiers of all unwholfome or tainted Air, and the moft excellent Prefervatives againft its noxious Influence; I fhall now endeavour to enforce the Inftructions I have given relating to them by Examples and Facts.

And here I muft obferve, it is the Cuftom of the Negroes in *Guinea*, as alfo of fome *Indians* (who both fleep for the moft Part on the Ground) to have a Fire, producing a little Smoak, conftantly burning in their Huts where they fleep. This not only corrects the

Moifture

Moisture of the Night, but also, by occasioning more Smoke than Heat, renders the Damp from the Earth less noxious. In all those unhealthful Places, particularly during Fogs or Rains, one is sensible of a raw Vapour, disagreeable to the Smell, which arises from the Earth, and especially in the Huts and Houses; of which, however, a little Smoke is the best Corrector. On this Occasion I was favoured by the Surgeon of a *Guinea-man* with the following Relation.

The Ship being up one of the Rivers for the Sake of Trade, it was found to be very dangerous to sleep on Shore; without which, their Trade could not so conveniently be carried on. First the Captain, then the Mate, and two or three of the Seamen were taken ill; each of them the Morning after they had lain on Shore. By these Accidents the Men were greatly intimidated from lying ashore; till the Surgeon boldly offered to try the Experiment on himself, which he did: and next Morning, when he waked, he found himself seized as the rest, with a Giddiness and Pain in the Head, &c. He immediately acquainted one of the Negroes with his Condition, who carried him to his Hut, and set him down in the Smoke of it; when his Shiverings and Giddiness soon left him. He then took a
Dram

Dram of the Bark Bitter; and found himſelf greatly relieved, eſpecially by breathing ſome Time in the Smoke. Thus inſtructed by the Negro, he ordered a large Fire to dry the Hut he ſlept in; and afterwards had every Night a ſmall Fire ſufficient to raiſe a gentle Smoke, without occaſioning a troubleſome Heat: and by theſe Means, he, and ſeveral others, uſing the ſame Precautions, ſlept many Nights on Shore without any Inconvenience. The Smoke was juſt ſufficient to deſtroy the Senſation of the raw damp Vapour uſual in ſuch Places.

But of all Vapours which infeſt the Torrid Zone, the moſt malignant and fatal are the *Harmattans:* And as I do not remember to have ſeen them any where deſcribed, I ſhall in this Place give the Relation I have had of them. They are ſaid to ariſe from the Conflux of ſeveral Rivers in the King of *Dormeo*'s Country at *Benin*; (the moſt unwholeſome Part of *Guinea*) where Travellers are obliged to be carried on Men's Backs for ſeveral Days Journey, through ſwampy Grounds, and over Marſhes, amidſt ſtinking Ooze, and Thickets of Mangrove Trees, which are annually overflown. Theſe Vapours come up the Coaſt as far as *Cape Mount*, a ſurprizing Extent of Country, with the S. E. and N. E. Winds:
And

And it has been observed, that, in their Progress, they have often changed both the Course of the Winds, and of the Sea-currents. The Times of their Appearance at *Cape Corsa* are, the Months of *December*, *January* or *February*. The N. E. and S. E. Winds are always unhealthy, but particularly so during the *Harmattan* Season. Some Years this Vapour is scarcely perceptible, but in others it is thick, noxious, and destructive to Blacks as well as white People. The Mortality is in Proportion to the Density and Duration of the Fog. It has a raw putrid Smell, and is sometimes so thick, that a Person or House cannot be discerned through it, at the Distance of fifteen or twenty Yards; and it continues so for ten or fourteen Days; during which it opens the Seams of Ships, splits and opens the Crevices of Wood, as if shrunk or dried by a great Fire, and destroys both Man and Beast. This was the Case in the Year 1754 or 1755, (I do not now recollect which it was said to be) when this noxious stinking Fog occasioned great Mortality in *Guinea*. I have been told, that in several Negro Towns, the Living scarce sufficed to remove or bury the Dead. Twenty Women brought over from *Holland* by a new Governor, to the Castle *del Mina*, all perished, together with most of the Men in the Garrison. The Gates of *Cape Corsa* Castle were shut up

for

for want of Centinels to do Duty; at this Time the Blacks dying as well as the Whites. The only Means that could be used during this Calamity, were firing Guns in the Castle, and burning every where pitched Staves, and the like; the Smoak of Fire always giving Relief. Several had Recourse to going on board the Ships in the Road, where the Vapour was less dense; and by the spreading of Awnings, and kindling of Fires, a Ventilation was procured more easily on the Water than on Shore. It is lucky, that it is only in some Years that *Harmattans* are so very thick and noxious, which would otherwise depopulate Part of the Country. It is observed that all Fogs are extremely unhealthy in those Parts, particularly before and after the rainy Season; and during those Times, the Smoak of Wood, pitched Staves, &c. are found to be the most proper Correctors of such an unhealthy Air. The *Tornado* Season is the most healthy on the *Guinea* Coast; those Hurricanes dispelling the Vapours, and purifying the Air.

But to return from this Digression. When Sickness begins to rage with a great Mortality amongst the Men, occasioned by lying in an unhealthful Harbour; in order to avoid the baneful Influences of the Land-Air, the

M   Ship

Ship muſt immediately put to Sea; there to ſeek and regain Health, as alſo the perfect Recovery of the Weak and Convaleſcent. This Expedient has often ſucceeded. Here the moſt material Point is, to take due Care of the ſick and weak that are brought on board. If they are immediately put on a groſs Sea-Diet, they will ſoon either become cachectic and dropſical, or die in the Flux; the latter being one of the moſt uſual Diſeaſes of hot Climates, as alſo the Conſequence of moſt others contracted there. I have been ſurprized to ſee ſo many Men arrive from the *Weſt Indies* reduced almoſt to Skeletons by this Malady. When a Ship puts to Sea with her Men for the Sake of Health, a proper Stock of the moſt light, nouriſhing, and reſtorative Food, ſhould always be carried out for thoſe who are ſick and weak; ſuch as *Goats* for Food, and Milk, *portable Soup*, *Eggs* preſerved by ſtopping up their Pores with Greaſe; Sago, and Salop, *Limes* and other *Fruits*, as alſo *Wine*, which is at all Times greatly preferable to Spirits of any Sort, but more eſpecially in the preſent Caſe. By ſuch Means the Sick will recover faſter at Sea than on Land.

This is the Sum of what I have to offer, as moſt likely to preſerve the Health of the Men in his Majeſty's Navy. But as it is proper to be provided against the worst that can befal, it is to be observed further,—That as soon as malignant, continued, remitting or intermitting Fevers and Fluxes make their Appearance at Sea, in close, hot and moist Weather, or are contracted by the unhealthful Air of a low, woody, marshy, sickly Country; a Tendency to Putrefaction seems to be produced in the animal Humours; and at such Seasons these Diseases are almost always to be suspected as infectious, more particularly the Bloody Flux. And then it is that the frequent Mortality and the speedy Progress of such Distempers in a Ship, are, for the most Part, more owing to Contagion, than to the Influence of any other Cause; the Air being more vitiated from thence than it possibly can be by any other Means. The Cloaths, Linen, Beddings, and various Utensils of the Sick, are apt to imbibe and propagate Contagion. And the Air of the sick Apartment, when in a close unventilated Place, becomes often so highly tainted, that I have known six Attendants infected by it in less than twenty-four Hours. Hence, also, often proceeds the uncommon Malignity and Mortality occasioned by Fevers, which we sometimes hear of in Ships.—There being Instances, where a Ship's Company have suffered as much in Proportion to their Number,

ber, by a Fever having acquired a high Degree of Malignity and Contagion from polluted Air, as any well-aired City would probably suffer by a Visit from the Plague, owing to a constant *Fomes* of Infection kept up in the Ship, from the want of due Precautions.

Thus it becomes a Matter of the utmost Consequence, to put in Execution all proper Methods for early stopping the Infection, and spreading of such Diseases; if any should unfortunately occur in a Voyage, as are plainly contagious.——To deliver a few Rules for that Purpose, was the second intended Branch of this Essay, to which I shall immediately proceed, after offering some Means of Relief in an unfortunate Situation, which I have not yet mentioned.

Bad Water is, next to bad Air, a frequent Cause of Sickness, especially of the Flux, in Places situated under the Torrid Zone. But as I have elsewhere* treated on bad Waters, and the Means of rendering them more wholesome, I shall here only give the following Advices. Where the Water is bad, the Casks should always be filled with Rain, when it can be done: Or, where there is Plenty of Fuel on Shore, the

---

* In my Book on the Scurvy.

the Sea Water may be diftilled, which will prove as wholefome as that of the *Thames* *.

If

* The Subftance of a Paper read before the Royal Society, being a Letter from Dr. *Lind* to Mr. R. h‑‑‑, Mafter of the Royal Academy at *Portfmouth*, and F.R.S.

"In revifing my Effay on preferving Seamen, there occurred to me a Diftrefs ufual to Mariners, which is the Want of good and wholefome Water in many Parts of the World at which they are obliged to remain.— A Calamity not indeed peculiar to Seamen, but to many of our Colonies and Factories abroad, who are deftitute of all other but the Rain Water. Whilft in other Places, especially on the *Guinea* Coaft, the bad Waters of the Soil are juftly fufpected to occafion Fluxes, the *Guinea* Worm, and various Maladies which infeft thofe Countries.

"In order to fupply fuch Places with a pure wholefome Water, and with the leaft Trouble, I have long meditated an Application of the Solar Fire for diftilling Sea-Water, upon the Principle, that though it was made greatly to exceed that of any Culinary or Furnace Heat, yet it would not melt any Metal fo long as Water uncompreffed was kept applied to its Side; and that various Contrivances might be made for retaining and diffufing it beyond the *Focus* of the *Speculum*.—As both the Glafs and Still fhould reft upon Stands, no farther Trouble would perhaps be requifite, than a Perfon to attend to bring back the burning *Focus* to its proper Line, when altered by the Sun's Motion.—And even to fave this Trouble a proper Apparatus might be thought of.

"But

If the Water, on digging a Pit in search of it, be found foul and impure, the Pit must be

" But previous to making any Trials by the Sun's Heat, I began with distilling Sea-Water, and various Ingredients, in order to fix upon such as would be least expensive, the most easy to be procured, and which would produce the purest elementary Water.

" I imagined that Sea Water distilled in Mr. *Appleby's* Way, had a soft Taste unnatural to Water. And I found upon distilling the Sea-Water from Soap-leys, Chalk, Lime, Ashes, &c. that each Ingredient communicated somewhat of its peculiar Taste and Flavour; but in no Distillation did the Sea Salt ascend in a greater Quantity than I found by a diluted Solution of Silver in Aqua Fortis to be contained in the Rain that usually falls here, near the Sea, when the Wind comes from thence.

" Being able to draw no certain Conclusions from the Distillations I had hitherto made to what Ingredients the Preference was due for distilling Salt Water fresh, and not having the Convenience of using Glass Retorts, I ordered a small Tin Still to be made, which should contain about two Quarts of Water, to be worked without a Worm-Tube in my Study.

" After properly cleansing this Still, I drew off some of the purest Rain Water, which I reserved as the standard Taste of a new distilled Water; or of any Flavour that might be imparted by the distilling Vessels. I then put some Sea-Water by itself into the Still, which, to my great Surprize, passed into the Receiver, without having any Mixture of *Bitumen* or Sea Salt, and, as I judged, equal in Purity to Rain Water.

" I

be made pretty deep and large, and its Bottom and Sides covered with large Stones, and then

" I tried it with a Solution of Salt of Lead, but found that neither it, nor indeed any diftilled Water, difcovers Impurities with this Solution, which is only proper to fearch for a *Selenites*.

" I obferved that when the Still run flow, the Sea-Water then boiling gently, the Water came over freer from Sea Salt than the rain Water aforementioned.

" I hope this Difcovery will prove ufeful, and I am,

" S I R,

Haflar Hofpital,
26 *April,* 1762.

" Your moft humble Servant,

" *James Lind.*"

Having found that when Sea-Water boils, nothing afcends but a pure Vapour, which when condenfed by any fimple Means, is converted into an excellent pure and elementary Water; no Perfons at Sea, or even when caft away upon a defert Ifland where there is Fuel, will now ever perifh for want of frefh Water, if either they carry a Still to Sea, or can on Shore make a Contrivance for diftilling fimply the Sea-Water.

The common Ship-boilers, by being fitted with a Pewter Still Head, will anfwer all the Purpofes of a Still at Sea. The Worm inftead of being placed in a Tub ftanding upon the Deck, may be contained in a clofe Cavity, furrounding this Head with a Receiver, hung or flung to the Extremity of its Pipe, that it may not be affected by the Ship's Motion. The cold Sea-Water fhould be poured into

then a considerable Quantity of clean dry Sand and Gravel may be thrown into it. By which

into this Cavity by a Funnel fixed at the Top, with a Valve to prevent the Effect of the Ship's rolling; and when it becomes hot, may either be conveyed by a Pipe into the Still, or allowed to run off by another Pipe filled with a Stop-cock. In Case of a Scarcity of Water at Sea, what Satisfaction it must afford to be possessed of the certain Means of Exemption from insufferable Thirst, Misery, and a cruel Death?

One would indeed think that the shocking Situation and Distress to which many Seamen and Passengers have been reduced for want of that invaluable Blessing, good Water, would induce all Commanders of Ships to be at the trifling Expence of so simple a Machine as this Head for their Pot or Coppers, and which would enable them at all Times to procure wholesome Water both for themselves, their Officers, Passengers, or Sick, in Place of their usual corrupt and stinking Water at Sea. A daily Supply of Water may be also procured without any additional Waste of Fuel.

Thus, if instead of Bricks, the Fire-places of Ships had Iron Pots fixed in such a Manner, that when the Fire was at any Time lighted to dress the Victuals, the Heat would be applied to the Side of the Iron Pots constituting the Side of the Grates, and consequently the Sea-Water contained in them being put into a boiling Heat, the Vapour might be condensed by such a simple Head to the Pots as has been described. By this means, in the worst Weather at Sea when it is possible to dress Victuals, a constant Supply of fresh Water for common Drink may be obtained.

Further,

which means the Water, will often become in twenty-four Hours, clear, soft, and wholesome.

But

Further, having recollected that Salt Pork in Ships, is always boiled in Sea-Water; as also Salt Beef in long Cruises or Voyages; and imagining, that if the Head of the Pots, in which those Provisions are dressed, were close and tight, those salted hard Meats might macerate and soften better, and there would be a considerable Saving of Fuel (as I found that Sea-Water boils with a less degree of Heat than fresh, and Water closely confined requires less Heat and Fuel to keep it boiling) I determined to make some Experiments on this Subject.

For this Purpose I took a Piece of Ship-salt Beef, another of salt Pork, and boiled each of them separately with Salt-Water, in a Pot with such a Still-head as hath been recommended at Sea. I was much pleased to find, that when salt Beef is boiled in Sea-Water, the condensed Vapour from the Pot (for none of it was allowed to escape) affords an excellent sweet Water, slightly tinctured with the Beef Flavour.

The Water got from Pork boiled in Sea-Water, had a stronger, though not disagreeable Flavour of Pork.

When the Beef and Pork were sufficiently boiled and very fresh, the Pot was emptied, and some Ship-Peas put into it with that Water only, which had been procured from the Sea in boiling the former flesh Meats. This Water was remarkably soft, and quickly softened, broke, and boiled the Peas. In like manner I boiled some Oatmeal with the same Water which made excellent Water-gruel.

Now

But if it still continues impure, let a small Cask, with both Ends struck out, be placed within

Now as both the Pease and Gruel were dressed in the same Pot as the Beef, with the condensing Cover, there was a Surplus of fresh Water, which originally came from the Sea, and upon standing twenty-four Hours, had neither Taste or Smell, but might serve either for a fresh boiling of Peas, or for the Use of the Hogs, Fowls, &c. in the Ship.

The whole usual Ship-provisions were thus dressed without the Use of any other but the Salt-Water, and an Overplus remained of wholesome fresh Water.

I am apt to think, that salt Beef will freshen equally well when boiled in Salt-Water as in the Fresh, provided the Water is renewed by letting the Brine occasionally run off by the Cock at the Bottom of the Copper, and supplying its Place with warm Sea-Water from the Refrigeratory.

When the Ship's Provisions are to be boiled, for saving Water in this Manner, the Pewter Head before recommended is to be used; and the Cook must be careful in keeping his Utensils very clean, and especially his Coppers free from Verdigrease.—Distilled Waters become much more palatable by keeping, and that got from the Sea will keep for many Months sweet in clean Vessels or Casks.

As to the Application of the solar Heat, it must be done to Sea-Water raised to a certain and known Level, in a close Iron or Tin Tube, and to a Part of that Tube in the Form of a truncated Cone, containing a

Quar-

within a larger Cask wanting the Head; then into both put some clean Sand and Gravel, so that the Level of the Sand in the inner Cask (sufficient Room being left to pour in Water) be higher than the Bed of Sand in the intermediate Space betwixt the two Casks: And in the outer Cask a Cock must be fixed above the Sand there, at a Level somewhat lower than the Surface of the Materials contained in the inner Cask.

By this Contrivance, the Water poured atop of the inner or small Cask, will sink through the whole Body of Sand, &c. in it; and passing also through the Gravel and Sand in the outer Cask, will ascend, and run off at the Cock.

Quart or two, or just as much Water as it is found, upon Tryal, that the burning Glass will set and keep boiling. —But further Experiments are requisite to evince the Utility of this last Method, and to put it in Practice.

I have only to add on this Subject, that it appears by some thermometrical Observations published in the Appendix, that Sea-Water when at Rest, freezes at ten Degrees below the freezing Point of fresh Water on *Farenheit*'s Thermometer. Whoever then discovers a Method of producing an artificial and constant Cold to that Degree, will be able to freeze Sea-Water, and consequently render it fresh and potable in the Cakes of Ice when thawed.

As the Surface of Sand in the inner Cask, becomes loaded with the grofs Impurities of the Water, it may be removed, and fresh Sand added. Or, for private Use, the Water may be strained through a large Funnel, having its narrow Mouth filled with a Bit of Spunge, above which is to be a Layer of Sand and Gravel, covered with a piece of Flannel, and over the whole another Layer of Sand. Care must be taken to change the Sand, Spunge, &c. as often as they are found to be loaded with the Impurities of the Water. By such means, pure and wholesome Water may frequently be procured from bad Wells.

Sand and Gravel are known to be fit for the Purposes abovementioned; when Water is poured upon them in a Vessel, and after stirring with a Stick, the same Appearances follow as in moving the Bed of a pure Rivulet, *viz.* upon removing the Stick, the Particles of small Sand instantly subside, and the Water stands on their Surface without having received any Tincture.

Some toasted Biscuits put into the Water of the River *St. Laurence*, were found serviceable in preventing the bad Effects of it in occasioning Fluxes in Sir *Charles Saunders's ders*'s Fleet. About four Pounds of burnt Biscuit were used to a Hogshead of Water.

I am informed that the Troops in *Canada*, for the same Purpose, mixed powdered Ginger with the bad Water, and found Benefit thereby.

At *Senegal*, where the Water is extremely unwholesome, unquenched Lime has been used to purify it.—But Water cannot thus be purified in a Ship, because I find that it must be exposed in a very wide mouthed Vessel for many Days, and sometimes Weeks, before it loses the Taste of the Lime: much of it is also expended, by daily removing the Scum; and it will sometimes require boiling.

The Addition of a small Quantity of Vinegar is likewise very proper, as an excellent Corrector of unhealthy Water; or Cream of Tartar, as before mentioned.

I shall conclude this Section with observing, that if any of the Directions hitherto given, cannot be complied with by all the Ship's Company, on account of their Number; they may notwithstanding be useful to many, such as Officers, and all others who have proper Convenience to execute them, and are desirous of of preferving Health and a good Conftitution, during their Refidence in an unhealthy Situation, efpecially under the Torrid Zone.

SECT. II.

Rules to be obferved for putting a Stop to the Spreading of contagious Difeafes.

A Point of great Importance, upon which the Recovery of the Afflicted, and the Prefervation of the Whole, will in a great meafure depend, is having a well-aired Hofpital or fick Berth, as it is commonly called in Ships, appropriated for the perfect Separation of the Difeafed from the Healthy; betwixt whom no common Intercourfe ought to be permitted. The Ufe of Ventilators muft at all Times greatly contribute to the general Health of the Ship; but on this Occafion they become indifpenfably neceffary, by affording a conftant Supply of frefh Air to the Sick, and a quick Diffipation of their morbid Steams. It is true, when once a contagious or peftilential Fever has invaded the Crew, the frefheft Air will not remove it; but then proper Ventilation may abate its Malignity, leffen the Mortality, which would otherwife be occafioned, and by carrying off and diffipating the contagious Effluvia of the Sick, become a great Means

Means of preventing its further Progress.—Another very material Advantage, derived from a constant Renewal of the Air, is, that in many Instances, this will prevent common Fevers, attended with no great Degree of Contagion, from becoming highly infectious. A Danger which is always to be apprehended, when there is a great and general Sickness on Board, as in any Part of the World an Infection may be quickly generated by the Effluvia of a Number of sick People closely confined, and who are not kept properly clean in their Linen, Beds, and Utensils, especially if they labour under Fevers, Fluxes, or other putrid Diseases.

Let us but reflect, that one Man in Health pollutes a Gallon of Air in a Minute, and by breathing, renders it unfit for the Purposes of Life. This is found to be the Case, by those who dive under Water, as by various other Experiments, and evinces the absolute Necessity of its constant Renovation; but more especially to Patients confined in Bed, as there is not any thing more refreshing, than the cool Air to the parched Lungs, or more essential to their Recovery, in every Species of Complaint*.

The

---

* Animals, even the most tenacious of Life, and those, whose Existence is found to depend the least on Air,

sooner

The Place commonly allotted for the Sick, is either the fore Part of the Gun-Deck, called the Bay, which is the moſt damp and unwholſome Part of a Ship; or, what is nearly as bad, and very incommodious, the fore Part of the Hold. Both theſe confined Places have too often proved a Seminary of Infection to her whole Company. If the Nature of the Service would permit, whenever the Dyſenteric or Tertian Fever, or other infectious Diſeaſe, more eſpecially the malignant and petechial, or what is called the Hoſpital Fever, are apprehended, the moſt proper Place for the Sick in warm Weather, or in a hot Climate, is under the Forecaſtle. They might there be ſufficiently defended from the Rain or Damps, by having Canvas hung round them, or a Partition made with Boards; and by this means all the Parts of the Ship below would be kept ſweet, clean and wholſome. If under the Forecaſtle ſhould be apprehended too noiſy, or deemed improper, as the Kitchen of the Ship, or otherwiſe thought incommodious; it is to be recollected, that this Advice is propoſed only to take Place on preſſing Occaſions, in a hot and calm Seaſon, when no other Device can be exerciſed, or Opportunity

---

ſooner expire in Air made foul, than in Vacuo. Plants ſooner ſuffer and droop beneath the Influence of noxious Steams, than in a Want of this vivifying Fluid.

had,

had, for separating the Sound from the Infected, with equal Advantage. That it is both practicable in some Ships, and has been of Use, the following is brought as a Proof.

In the Year 1751, a Ship of twenty Guns in the *Mediterranean* was infected by a Fever, which, in the Course of four Months, attacked 70 of her Men; who were all, as is usual, subject to frequent Relapses, whilst they lay below: But upon removing the Sick under the Forecastle, the Disease soon disappeared, and in that Place they did not lose a Man.

But supposing this Place is at any time found to be inconvenient, from the Number of the Sick, or their incommoding the Working of the Ship, &c. the Patients ought then to be removed into the Gun-Room, for the Benefit of that salutary Draught of Air, which may be constantly procured them, by keeping open the Gun-Room-Ports. The Objection of the greatest Weight that can well be made against this Step, is, the Inconvenience which may arise from it to the Officers who eat and sleep in that Part. But how trifling must this Objection appear, when offered against the most proper Means of preserving their own, and many other Lives? It ought to be considered, that the Necessity of taking this

this Method, will but rarely occur. Many Ships continue for Years as healthy in the *Weſt-Indies*, as they would in *Portſmouth* Harbour, eſpecially after being ſeaſoned a little to that Climate.

There is ſeldom Occaſion to remove the Sick in a Ship, from their proper Beds, into one Place; and it is done only, when their Number is encreaſed, ſo as to make it inconvenient for other Men to attend them in ſeparate Parts. Now after this Step is firſt taken, and a proper Berth between Decks, or in the Hold, has been provided, where the Ventilators and other Means have been uſed, and yet notwithſtanding this, becauſe of the the daily Encreaſe of the Sick, the Progreſs of the Mortality, and the plainly contagious Nature of the Diſeaſe, more Air, and a ſpeedy Removal from an infected Berth, are found to be abſolutely requiſite; I believe, there are few Officers in the *Engliſh* Service, who would not willingly quit their Habitation in the Gun-Room, for the Benefit and Preſervation of the Men. And this is only to be done, until they arrive in Port, and the Diſeaſed are landed.

Let it be remembered, that if an Infection is in a Ship, Officers have no Security againſt it, it, by sleeping in the Gun-Room; on the contrary, if they are permitted to have Hammocks in the *Steerage*, they are there much safer. The absolute Security of all on board does indeed entirely depend upon a Stop being put, without Delay, to the Progress of the Contagion.

'Tis further to be recollected, that such well-aired Places as the Gun-Room, by the Methods hereafter mentioned, are much easier cleansed from all Infection, when the Diseased are once removed, than the other more confined and constantly damp Parts of the Ship.

If it is still objected, that the Effluvia from the Sick would, by means of the Air entering at the Gun-Room Ports, be carried to other Parts of the Ship; I answer, there is no Danger of this, if the Place and Patients are kept sufficiently clean and neat. But effectually to prevent the least Suspicion of this Inconvenience, a perfect Separation may be made of the Gun-Room from the other Parts of the Ship, by a Partition made with Boards or painted Canvass, nailed up. If after all that has been said, the Gun-Room is not permitted for the Use of the Sick; an Hospital in the Bay is to be acquiesced in, which ought to have Air-Holes or Scuttles cut on each Side, as also a Pipe of the Ventilator, to be played when the Weather will not permit the Air-Scuttles to be kept open.

Too much cannot well be said to conquer the Prejudices of the Ignorant, who are unacquainted with the pernicious Effects of confining Patients, labouring under a contagious Illness, in a foul stagnating Air. In such a Case, the Malignity of the Fever hourly acquires Strength from the pent-up Steams of the Diseased; and those morbid Effluvia are imbibed by all the surrounding Materials, even the Timber itself: From whence a strong Source of Infection is formed in such Apartments, constantly emitting poisonous Steams. In such a polluted Air, and tainted Apartment, the most powerful Antidotes, and febrifuge Remedies, lose their Efficacy.

The Attendants on the Sick, the Surgeon and his Mates, cannot well escape, and are often, in their Turn infected. Even those, who at first have had the good Fortune to recover, have no Security against a Relapse, their Continuance in such a tainted Air will almost certainly effect it.—More Danger is doubtless to be apprehended to the Sick, from breathing in an Air polluted with their own and the
Effluvia

Effluvia of others, than from any Degree of Cold, which can well be admitted by fresh Air.

When a great Number are crowded in the Gun-Room, they will require the Ports to be open Day and Night, only it may be requisite to have Canvas Shutters, to prevent too much Cold in bad Weather. It is here taken for granted, that the Patients are duly supplied at this Time, with sufficient clean, and, if necessary, warm Bedding.

This Apartment assigned to the Sick, ought to be kept free from all Incumbrances of Chests and the like; as also from Crowds of People. It must be washed out every Day with warm Vinegar, sprinkling the Sides of the Ship, and the Beams above the Hammocks. All possible Care must be taken during this Operation, that the Patients be not kept too close or stifled up. The Utensils of the Sick ought also to be washed or sprinkled with Vinegar, especially the necessary Buckets, when the Men are afflicted with the Dysentery. In this Case, the Buckets, immediately after using, must be washed, and afterwards have warm Vinegar poured into them.

For

For further Security, frequent Fumigation is also requisite, as a necessary Means for the more certain Purification or Emendation of the Air. The Fumes of camphorated Vinegar, of Nitre, of Pitch, Tar, and the like, will be found serviceable. But what I would chiefly advise, is to burn two or three Times a Day, in different Parts of the Ship, a small Quantity of wetted Gun-Powder, secured in a proper Vessel. But more of this hereafter.

What Dr. *Huxham* has recommended to several Ships, and has been found very beneficial, is a Decoction of Chamomile Flowers, Rosemary, Gum Myrrh, Roses, and Camphire in sharp Vinegar. It must be kept boiling in a proper Vessel over a Stove for the Purpose, whence it diffuses a very strong and pleasant Fume. Such Fumes or Smoke ought every Day to be renewed, and their Use continued so long as the Sickness subsists *.

---

* I have lately observed again and again with Pleasure, the excellent Effects of Fumigation, when repeated and persisted in for some Time, to remove very bad infectious Fevers from the Prison-Ships in *Portsmouth* Harbour, and the *French* Prison at *Forton*. For it is not to be expected that once or twice fumigating will destroy an Infection in a Ship or Prison where a Number of Persons are confined and sickly.

With

With regard to those who are diseased, much will depend upon their being kept as clean as possible, Filthiness being a chief Source of Infection, and Cleanliness an excellent Preservative. The less cleanly may have their Hands and Feet washed with a little warm Water and Soap, or with Vinegar. When their Linen becomes foul and stiff with sweating, they ought directly to be shifted, and after fumigating such foul Linen with Smoke of Brimstone, they should be soaked in Vinegar, and washed. Dry fresh Bedding is a great Comfort to sick Persons. Every Bed, as soon as the Patient is recovered so far as to be able to get out of it, should be carried upon Deck, and there be well fumigated, aired, dried and beat by his Mess-Mate.

It is needful also that there be a Recovery-Place or Berth, into which the Convalescents are to be soon removed, taking Care that the Cloaths and Bedding be sufficiently cleaned and fumigated before their Admission into it.

This Regulation, enjoined by the Commanding Officer, ought to take Place every Day at Noon, when the Weather will permit, *viz.* That all the empty Beds in the Hospital be carried upon Deck and well aired, and if needful, smoaked and dried. Some Sailors, from a natural slovenly Disposition, and others, when weak after Illness, are apt to be very remiss in this Point of Cleanliness, which however ought not to be in their Power to neglect. Such Beds as are observed to be quite spoiled and rotten, must be destroyed, and supplied by issuing new ones to the Men; as ought likewise the Beds of all those who have laboured under the Dysenteric Fever, because the Bedding in this and some other Fevers, and indeed most Substances of a loose, spungy Texture, such as Wool, Feathers, &c. do strongly retain, and are apt to communicate the Contagion afresh.

The Sick are to be placed at a convenient Distance from each other, so as not to be too much crowded. Those who have Fluxes, putrid Sores, scorbutic Ulcers, and the like offensive Ailments, (which in a confined Place are sufficient of themselves to pollute the Air, and to generate a Contagion) are to be put in the best-aired Place of the Apartment; or rather removed into a separate Place, under the Forecastle or Half-deck. Such as are under a Salivation for Venereal Diseases, are not to be admitted into the sick Apartment. Nor is this Place to be crowded with Men, labouring under any slight Complaint, or indeed any other Disease, than the reigning Epidemic one, if

this

this be infectious.—Dead Bodies ought without Delay to be removed upon Deck, and the Bedding and Body-Linen of the Deceased to be thrown into the Sea. The best and sweetest Water in the Ship should always be reserved for the Use of the Sick, especially in putrid and dysenteric Cases *.

For the thorough Purification of the Ship, Fires made of dried Wood sprinkled with any resinous Substance, such as Pitch, boiled Turpentine, and the like, and moved succeslively into all the different Parts below, have been found very beneficial. When these Fires are brought near the Sick, the Ports must all be thrown open, as too much Heat has always been suspected of dangerous Influence in infectious Fevers; and therefore every Method is to be used, during this Operation, of keeping the Men agreeably cool in their Beds, whilst the rest are sent upon Deck.

As Wood Fires, which I had formerly † recommended, have, by late Experience in the Fleet, been found so effectual in preserving the

* For more particular Directions concerning the Treatment of the Patients on board of Ships, See Dr. *Lind*'s Treatise on the Scurvy. Part II. Chap. 3.

† Treatise on the Scurvy, Ed. 2. p. 185.

Health of the Men, and in purifying a tainted Air, it is needful to relate their Effects. The common Observation is, that after a Ship has been for some Time in bad Weather with the Hatchways shut, the Air below, notwithstanding all the Means that can be used, is found to be close and disagreeable; doubtless from the damp Effluvia constantly emitted from all the various Contents there: But after the Purification by Wood Fires, or of burnt pitched Staves, the Heat of which goes quickly off with proper Ventilation by the Ports, Wind-Sails, &c. the Air becomes quickly much cooler than before, and continues in all the lower and unventilated Parts of the Ship sensibly fine, cool, and pleasant for some Days afterwards. Thus it would seem that Fire consumes tainted Air, and renders it cooler and fresher, after the Extinction of the Heat, by the Purification of all damp and polluted Substances.

This Observation hath been sufficiently verified by repeated Experience.

The next Things to be considered, are the Means, by which particular Persons may best defend themselves against Contagion; and it is upon this Occasion, that a Glass of the Bark-Bitter taken once or twice a Day, will be
found

found an excellent Preservative against Sickness and Infection.—This may be presumed from what has been already said, and has further been confirmed by repeated Experience in like Cases. The learned Dr. *Pringle* has described, under the Denomination of the Hospital Fever, an Infection of a most virulent and high Degree; to whom the World is greatly indebted for some excellent Observations on that, and on many other Diseases, incident in a great Measure to the Fleet, as well as to the Army. This Gentleman, by a lucky Accident, discovered the Efficacy of the Bark in this Malignant Fever. " * Even after the " Recess of the Fever, the same Medicine " (*viz.* a Decoction of the Bark and Snake- " Root) being continued in a smaller Quan- " tity, not only served as a Strengthener, but " likewise as a Preservative against a Re- " lapse, whilst the Patient remained in the " Hospital." These Observations, which agree with what other Practitioners, particularly the learned Doctor *Huxham* † remarked in

---

* Observations on the Diseases of the Army.

† I cannot but upon this Occasion recommend to the Surgeons of the Royal Navy, the Perusal of the following excellent Books, *viz.* All the Writings of Dr. *Huxham*, particularly his Essay on Fevers, and Dr. *Pringle*'s Observations on the Diseases of the Army. For the remitting

in like Cafes, are now added, as corroborative Proofs of the prefervative Virtues of the Bark. And I further recommend it to the Trial of all Nurfes and Attendants on or about the Sick at Land, for their proper Security againſt Infection. We often obferve a Fever to run thro' a whole Family, and even the next Neighbours to become infected by it; the Precautions here directed, together with the Bark, are the beſt Prefervatives I know *.

For perfect Security in an Affair of fuch Importance, where there is a ſtrong Infection, either at Sea or Land, the Surgeons, for their own proper Prefervation, muſt take Care never to vifit the Sick when their Stomachs are empty, the Body being then in an abforbing State, nor after a full Meal of hard, and not eafily digeſted Food. The moſt eligible Seafon is

mitting Autumnal Fever of hot Countries, they may confult *Cleghorn* on the Difeafes of *Minorca*, Dr. *Grainger de febre Anomala Batava*, and likewife Dr. *Pringle*'s Obfervations.

* At *Haflar* Hofpital I have experienced a Decoction of the Bark very efficacious in preventing Relapfes into infectious Fevers: But it will fometimes fail, when the Patient commits great Irregularities, or is expofed to ſtrong infectious Caufes. However, this detracts no more from its Efficacy in fuch Cafes, than its failing fometimes to cure obſtinate Agues, as is well known to Practitioners.

after

after a light Breakfast of Tea, or the like; and a Slice of toasted Bread dipt in Vinegar, or rather the Bark-Bitter, may be taken a very little Time before entering into the Sick Chamber; and the Mouth afterwards washed with camphorated Vinegar, swallowing a little of it with the Spittle. The Nostrils may be stopped with a little Lint dipped in the same Vinegar, which I have often used in the Hospital, in so small a Roll as not to be perceived by the Sick. A Suit of Cloaths which is reserved for the Purpose ought then to be put on. And it is to be remembered that Linen Stuffs, especially waxed ones, are preferable to woollen Materials. If convenient, at this Time the Sick-chamber should be fumigated by some purifying Steam of Tar (which is excellent) or the like Substances: The Effect of which will be, that to remove this Smoke, some Inlet of Air will be opened, by which the Chamber will become perfectly ventilated and refreshed. These Precautions being premised (all of which need only be used in Cases of the most dangerous Infection, either in a House, Ship, or Hospital) a Person may freely, and ought with great Confidence enter any infected Place, or Chamber, at the same time chewing somewhat which may occasion him to spit often, and some warm camphorated Vinegar may be held at Times

Times betwixt him and the Patient, of which he may receive the Steam; as alſo dip his Finger in the Vinegar before feeling the Pulſe, and afterwards, if any diſagreeable Senſation remains. A Spunge is not to be uſed on this Occaſion for wetting the Fingers, or other Purpoſes, at leaſt more than once in a Place that is truly infected. After the neceſſary Buſineſs is performed, upon going into another Chamber, or into the freſh Air, the Mouth is again to be waſhed with camphorated Vinegar, the Noſe-plugs removed, the Cloaths ſhifted, and the Hands waſhed. As I have often had Opportunities of viſiting Patients labouring under the moſt contagious Diſeaſes at *Haſlar* Hoſpital, and never was in the leaſt affected; ſo I may venture to ſay, that if the above Precautions are ſeverally uſed, no great Danger will ariſe from viſiting Caſes of the moſt peſtilential Nature: But to return to the Subject of Infections in a Ship. Vinegar and Garlic, no contemptible Preſervatives, ſhould at this Time be ſerved to the Men, by Way of Sauce for their Salt-Meats. Furniſhing them alſo with Pipes and Tobacco, and making them ſmoke freely, has been a Method often practiſed with Succeſs in different Ships.

It is obſervable, that the Perſpiration and Sweat of the Patient are infectious in many Fevers,

Fevers, but above all the Stools: the Breath of a dying Person is bad, and all Fevers have been esteemed to be most contagious towards their latter End. Swallowing the Spittle in infected Places is justly deemed a Means of sooner acquiring the Taint; upon which Account, neither the Nurses, nor any one else, should be suffered to eat in the Hospital. The Wine, before directed to be reserved for the Use of the Sick, will at such a Season be found extremely beneficial, not only as the best Medicine in certain Stages of the Fever, but as an excellent Strengthener and Preservative of the Convalescents. All spirituous Liquors moderately used, as also Lemons, are approved Prophylactics against Contagion. Wine is perhaps inferior to none of these*. If it is found inconvenient to serve the whole Ship's Company with Wine, their Allowance of Punch (made as before directed) may be encreased. Or, if this cannot well be done,

---

* A Glass of Wine, with the Juice of half a Lemon, and Sugar, taken before visiting or bleeding the Sick, I also recommend as an experienced efficacious Preservative against Contagion in infected Places. It is usual with some, for preventing their swallowing Spittle, to put Tobacco in their Mouths when attending about the Diseased; but those who are in constant Use of chewing that Plant, are apt to let down Part of its Juice with their Saliva. I would advise such Persons to use a Slice of the Root of *Calamus Aromaticus*, dipt in Vinegar, and spit often.

the Nurses ought at least to be permitted such a Quantity more than their ordinay Allowance, as may be judged reasonable to prevent their Sickness, without endangering their Abuse of it.

It will import much to the Health of all the Attendants about the Sick, that they keep both themselves and their Patients perfectly clean, and free from Filth and Nuisances; a Rule of great Consequence in a Ship. If the Attendants on the Sick wore painted Canvas-Jackets, they would be less liable to carry about Infection, and the like Method should be taken with their Linen, as has been directed for those of the Sick. I must add, the most chearful and willing Men ought always at such Times to be preferred as Attendants on the Diseased; Grief and Fear, being experienced greatly to dispose the Body to receive Impressions, which Mirth and Gaiety might resist. Universal Chearfulness, good Humour, and entertaining Amusements, with moderate Exercise, should be enjoined and promoted by the Officers on board. Great Fatigue of Body, Irregularities of every Sort, especially Surfeits and Drunkenness, as also long Fasting, ought carefully to be avoided, especially at such a Time as we now suppose.

It

It is a received Opinion, that *Fear* is a Cause of itself sufficient to produce, in certain Dispositions, a bad or malignant Fever. There are at least many Instances in besieged Towns, where no other Reason could be well assigned for the Rise of malignant Disorders, than the Dejection of Spirits, Grief, and Panic of the Inhabitants, occasioned by the Bombardment, and the Apprehensions of a violent Death from some sudden Assault of the Enemy. This much is certain, that such Passions of the Mind serve powerfully to propagate an Infection, even the Plague itself. So that on all such Occasions, too much Art cannot be used to animate, with Hope and Confidence, both the Afflicted and the Sound. Spectacles of Horror are never to be exposed to the View of sick Persons: those, therefore, who die, should be removed silently and privately out of an Hospital to a proper Place, where no idle Spectators should be permitted to view the ghastly Appearance. It is always to be remembered, that every Ceremony that is observed relating to a Corpse, makes a deep Impression on the Mind, especially of the afflicted and dispirited; and by such Impressions the Body is surprisingly affected.

If any should think that the many Precautions I have mentioned are trifling, it is for fear they may be thought so, that they are so particularly inculcated.

Upon the first Appearance of Sickness in an Attendant, which may be judged to have arisen from his being employed in the sick Berth, he is not immediately to be confined there, or to have his Hammock hung among the rest; as I have observed many Instances, where sudden Infection, from bad Air, has gone quickly off, by Means of a gentle Vomit given without Delay, and afterwards a thorough Sweat.

It remains for me to lay down a few of the most proper Directions for purifying the Ship, and preventing the latent Seeds of a contagious Fever from breaking out again, after all the Sick, upon the Ship's Arrival at Port, are sent away to the Hospital. These are the more needful, as Experience in Ships has shewn, that the getting quit of their Sick, has not always cleared them of their Infection.

On the first good Day, after the Diseased are removed, together with their Cloaths, and the Gun-Powder put on Shore, Charcoal Fires, first sufficiently kindled upon Deck, must be carried below, and there sprinkled with Brimstone; the Steam of which must be pretty closely confined for some Time. Afterwards all

all the Bedding and Cloaths muſt be ordered on the Poop or Quarter-Deck, when the Ship rides with her Head to the Wind. There the Cheſts are to be opened, and the Bedding ſpread out; taking Care, that whatever is of Cotton, Wool, or Feathers, be well dried and beat, and that no Folds remain unexpoſed to the free Air. A gentle Breeze upon this Occaſion will be ſerviceable. At the ſame Time, the Quarters of the Men below are to be waſhed out by Means of the Fire-Engine, if there be one on Board. This Engine, by throwing the Water with a confiderable Force againſt the Sides of the Ship, cleanſes the ſeveral ſmall Holes and Crevices of the Timbers, much better than the Hand-Buckets.—Every Hammock in the Ship ought now to be well waſhed and ſcrubbed, as alſo the Men's Cheſts, which are often very offenſive, from the Remains of rotten Cheeſe, mouldy Bread, and other Articles of their Proviſions.

This firſt neceſſary Step of Cleanlineſs being premiſed, every Part of the Ship muſt afterwards be waſhed out with warm Vinegar. It may be done by the moſt lazy, indolent, and leſs cleanly Fellows, ſuch as have either recovered of the Sickneſs, or may be deemed liable to it from a Neglect in Point of Cleanlineſs: The old Cloaths of thoſe Perſons are at this Time either to be purified with Vinegar, &c. or deftroyed.

All this being duly performed, makes Way for the burning of Gun-powder. I will venture to affirm, that of the many Fumes recommended for the Emendation of the Air, and the Purification of infected Places and Subftances, none are more effectual to eradicate an Infection out of a Ship, or indeed any other Place, than the confined Smoke of Gunpowder. This I affirm from Experience, without laying any Strefs upon the different Materials, Sulphur, Nitre, &c. which enter into the Compofition of this falutary Vapour. The Manner is this:—All the Chefts, Cloaths, and Bedding of the Men, are to remain below, the Ports, Hawfe-holes and Hatch-ways being kept clofe fhut, whilft fmall Quantities of Gunpowder are fired in different Parts of the Hold and between Decks. A Pafte may be made by thoroughly wetting the Gunpowder with Water. A fmall Portion of this Pafte is to be thrown at a Time into the Bottom of a broad and deep Ladle, or an old Kettle or Saucepan containing live Coals, fufficiently fecured by ftanding in a deep Bucket, or large Tub of Water. This Precaution, with that of throwing only very fmall Quantities at a Time of loofe Powder on the wet Pafte to

promote

promote its taking Fire, will effectually secure against any Danger.—The Operation is to be repeated, as long as the Operators below can stand the Smoke, (which by the bye, is quite harmless to the Lungs) and, until the Hold and all the Parts between Decks, are sufficiently replete with it.—They ought to set Fire to their last Train, just as they leave the Gun-Deck in ascending the last Ladder, when the Hatchway, by which they came up, is without Delay to be shut, and, like the others, well covered over with a tight tarred Canvas Covering. The Smoke must be confined below for at least two Hours, until all the Contents of the Ship, the Timbers, Bedding, Cloaths, &c. are sufficiently penetrated and purified with this antiseptic Vapour.——The Hatch-ways are afterwards to be opened, and a Spring being put on the Cable, the Hawse-holes are to be brought to the Wind; so that by this Means, the Ship (having her Gun-Room-Ports thrown open, or whatever else will encrease the Current) may receive a full Stream of fresh and wholesome Air throughout her darkest Recesses, which ought also to be well purified, by playing of the Ventilators.

I observed I had Experience of the Efficacy of Gun-powder; and, indeed, I have known some

some sickly *Guinea* Ships, perfectly purified and rendered wholesome by the Smoke of it, when other Methods had been tried in vain. I must now add, that in all contagious Diseases and infected Places, in Hospitals or Chambers of the Sick at Land, it is a most excellent Purifier.

When the Ship is quite cleared of all its Contents, more especially if it be a new Vessel, Fires made of dry Woods, such as Pine, Fir, &c. of Herbs, such as Juniper, Rosemary, or the like, may be kindled in proper Vessels in the Hold, and occasionally bestrewed with Tobacco, tarred Rope, or even Brimstone. These Fires must be kept smoaking and burning for a considerable Time in different Parts of the Ship. By these Means the most infected Vessels, Prisons, &c. may be thoroughly purified.

In so serious a Matter, indeed, too many Precautions cannot well be taken to accomplish the entire Purity of a Ship; and this is the Reason why, in the preceding Pages, I have given a Detail of so many different Processes. When the Nature of the Service will permit it, a sickly infected Ship ought to remain at least thirty Days in Port, in order to judge of the future State of the Men's Health. None
who

who have laboured under the Fever ſhould be received on board of her, for at leaſt fourteen Days after their perfect Recovery, as one Perſon, tho' ſeemingly well, may perhaps be the Occaſion of again introducing a general Sickneſs.

I muſt add, ſound healthy Ships ought to be extremely cautious upon this Head, of what Men they receive from infected Hoſpitals, or from ſickly Ships. For want of this Precaution many have ſuffered. To produce one from ſeveral Inſtances.——I remember in the Time of the late War, upon the Arrival of a Dutch Man of War at *Spithead*, from the *Weſt-Indies*, that two *Engliſh* Men on board of her, petitioned that they might be taken out, as being *Britiſh* Subjects, and willing to ſerve in the *Engliſh* Fleet. Their Requeſt was preſently granted, and accordingly they came on board one of our Ships, without having any Appearance of Sickneſs; but next Morning one of them was found in a Fever, and the other dead in his Bed. This Fever turned out to be highly contagious, and annoyed our Fleet for ſome Time afterwards.——I have mentioned this Fact, to enforce the Neceſſity of proper Precaution, and to evince the Importance of many Directions which have been here delivered.

When

When a Veſſel is annoyed with Rats, Mice, or Inſects uſual in the *Weſt-Indies*, ſuch as Ants, Cock-Roaches, Weevils, and thoſe of the Beetle Kind, which encreaſe Impurity, particularly in the moſt important of Articles, the Food; the burning of Sulphur may be practiſed, Care being taken to extract the ſulphureous Air, before the Men are permitted to go below. Another needful Caution is, that the Fire be at firſt gentle to draw the Rats towards it, that ſo they may be ſtifled in the Hold by the Smoke there, and not at once ſuffocated by a quick and violent Steam, when dying and afterwards rotting betwixt the Ship's Timbers, they are apt, for a conſiderable Time afterwards, to occaſion a poiſonous and noxious Stench.

With regard to Naval Hoſpitals, two Things I conceive may prove beneficial.

Firſt, it ſhould be ordered by a Regulation in the Navy, that when a Ship arrives from a Cruize or Voyage, having either a malignant, ſpotted, or dyſenteric Fever, or any other Diſeaſe on board, which is plainly contagious, that, in this Caſe, the Captain or Surgeon ſhould acquaint the Phyſician, Surgeon, or Director of the Hoſpital, with their Condition, previous to the Landing of the Sick, that

that proper and distinct Wards may be prepared for their Reception.—The ordinary Method has been, that as soon as the Ship is brought to an Anchor, the Sick are often sent on Shore, in the first Boats, to the Hospital, and are dispersed into the different Wards, according as the Beds are found empty, without any Information given to the Surgeon of the Nature of their Disease, till he receives the sick Ticket, which is carried along with them.

As I have hitherto endeavoured to support, by Facts, what has been advanced, so I cannot but observe, that, for want of this proposed Regulation, more than once it happened, during the late War, that a few Men, put on Shore from a foul Ship, have introduced a Contagion into an Hospital, containing a thousand Sailors.—This was the Case both at *Gibraltar* and *Mahon* Hospitals, where the Fever diffused itself so, as to endanger the Inhabitants, and especially the Garrison of the former Place. Nay more, these Hospitals became a Seminary of Contagion to the whole Fleet, as I experienced in a very healthy Ship, the *Kennington*, where, by taking on board but one recovered Man from the Hospital, the Fever was introduced among us, and afterwards exerted its Contagion for six Months.

The other Regulation is a Consequence of the former, *viz.*—That, in all Hospitals, there should be separate Wards allotted for different Diseases. As no Man ought to be received into the Hospital, without the previous Inspection of the Surgeon, so it must be his Business to appropriate Places to each; and in Case of the Arrival of a Ship, with a contagious Fever on board, as above-mentioned, he is then to prepare distinct Wards for the Reception of the Men; and to use all proper Methods, for preventing the Contagion from affecting the rest of the Sick.——Many Precepts for this Purpose have been already delivered, so that I shall only say, the foul Wards in an Hospital ought always to be the best aired, and, where the Contagion is eminently malignant, spacious Tents with Fire-places, built in the Fields adjoining, are greatly preferable to any close Ward or Apartment, for dissipating Infection, and for the Recovery of the Diseased.

When a malignant Fever, in the late War, was brought from *England* into the Hospital at *Mahon*, the House being found insufficient for the Reception of so great a Number of Patients,

tients, Tents were erected in the Fields for many of the Men. These poor Men were thought to be badly accommodated, but it was very observable, that most of those, who lay in the Tents, recovered; when the Mortality in the House was so great, that in some Wards, not one in three escaped. This occurred in a hot Climate, and in Summer.

Thus I have drawn a Picture, at full Length, of the Mischiefs that may possibly flow from want of due Care and Circumspection, with a View to excite the Attention of such as might be negligent in Matters of so serious a Concern. The Province has been mine to deliver Precepts; the Power is in others to execute; and if the Expedients proposed, are thought by some, either too numerous or troublesome, let it be remembered, that to oppose the various Evils, to which our Fleets, and consequently the Safety of these Kingdoms, stand exposed, we should, with united Efforts, attempt to intercept every Reinforcement which may tend to strengthen Disease. For notwithstanding every Chance and Assistance on the Side of human Art, the unavoidable Inconveniencies of Noise, Motion, crowded Numbers, and the comparative Want of Accommodations, will ever render Indisposition aboard a much superior Calamity to similar Diseases ashore. Hence the Necessity of being, in this precautionary Tract, so circumstantial and minute.—But it is full Time to close these Scenes, and glance on what may afford a great Portion of Comfort and Encouragement.

The Seamen, on board his Majesty's Ships of War, have not only a fuller and more wholesome Diet allowed them, than in any other Service, but also an excellent Provision of the most proper Necessaries of all Sorts for the Afflicted.—Their Surgeons, in general, are now well qualified, and the Sick have at all Times a sufficient Number of careful Attendants, to administer due Assistance in their Distress. They are likewise commonly less crowded with Men, than foreign Ships of War; and in every Respect better provided with Assistance, and all the necessary Comforts in Sickness, than Merchant Ships can possibly be. Hence it is, that in Proportion to the Number of Men on board, they are often much healthier; for, from the *Guinea* and *West-India* Traders, the King's Ships have sometimes contracted their Sickness.

In the Merchant's Service, the Condition of the poor Mariner, when at Sea, is often much

much to be pitied, where he is deftitute of proper Advice and Affiftance, and even of fuch Neceffaries as might afford a prefent momentary Relief, and render his Affliction more tolerable.——In many Cafes, when in Harbour, the Men are obliged to expend a great Part of their Wages for a Cure; which, in his Majefty's Service, they might have compleated by fome of the moft able Phyficians and Surgeons without Expence. This is an Encouragement beyond what fome other Nations give; for thofe who are in the *French* King's Ships (if I am rightly informed) have all their Pay ftopped, when in the Hofpital, or under Cure.——Nor is it a fmall additional Pleafure to a Seaman in the Royal Navy, to reflect, that whatever Misfortunes, incident to his Way of Life, may befal him in the Service of his Country, he will be honourably rewarded, and, under many Circumftances of but fmall Accident, obtain a Penfion for Life.

APPENDIX.

HAVING had Occasion already to observe, that Blood-letting, by Way of Prevention from Diseases, on passing the Tropic of Cancer, was an usual Practice at Sea*, it may not be altogether foreign to the Purpose of this Essay, to subjoin a few general Remarks on that Operation, for the Benefit of those, who never practised in the Torrid Zone. The Observations may perhaps be found the more necessary, as unexperienced Practitioners are apt to imagine the Principles they have been taught, relating to Diseases in *Europe*, may serve for invariable Rules of Practice in all other Climates.

It was before observed, that a Transition, especially if quick, from cold to extreme hot

* See Page 47.

Weather, generally induces a plethoric Difpofition. The Signs are, a Pain and Giddinefs of the Head, a Heavinefs and Dullnefs of the Eyes; fometimes the *Tunica Conjunctiva* appears flightly inflamed, there is ufually a Senfe of Fullnefs and Weight in the Breaft, the Pulfe feeling quick and oppreffed. Some, at this Seafon, are feized with ardent Fevers; a few with Diarrhœas. In fuch Cafes, plentiful Blood-letting is plainly indicated.

But the Cafe is quite different, after a longer Continuance of fultry Weather, and when the Conftitution is in fome Meafure habituated to the hot Climate. For 'tis then obferved, that the Symptoms of Topical Inflammations in the Bowels, even the moft dangerous, are not near fo fevere in fuch Climates, as in cold Countries; nor can the Patients bear fo large Evacuations. The Practitioner, however, is not to be mifled by the Mildnefs of the Symptoms; for he will find, notwithftanding fuch deceitful Appearances, that the Inflammation makes a more rapid Progrefs in hot Countries, than in cold; Suppurations and Mortifications being much more fuddenly formed; and that, in general, all acute Diftempers come fooner to a Crifis in the Southern than in colder Regions. Hence it is an important Rule of Practice in thofe Climates, to feize the

the moſt early Opportunity in the Commencement of all threatening Inflammations, to make frequent, though not copious, Evacuations by Blood-letting. For, by Delay, the Inflammation ſwiftly paſſes from its firſt to its laſt or fatal Stage; at leaſt an imperfect Criſis in ſuch inflammatory Fevers enſues, which fixes an Obſtruction in the Parts or Viſcera, extremely difficult to remove.

It is indeed a general Maxim with ſome of our *Engliſh* Practitioners in the *Weſt Indies*, that, in moſt acute Diſtempers, Bleeding in that Country is prejudicial. This is founded upon a Suppoſition, that the *Craſſamentum* of the Blood is too much reſolved, and the Solids greatly weakened by the Heat of the Climate. So, ſay they, when a Fever is contracted, either from an Error in the Non-naturals, or by the epidemical Conſtitution of the Seaſon, Bleeding, in ſuch a State of the Habit, by debilitating the Powers of Nature, withdraws that Strength from the Body, which is requiſite to ſupport the Patient until the Criſis is accompliſhed. The Reaſoning is partly juſt; yet, like a general Maxim, will admit of many Exceptions.

Firſt, with regard to Sailors, it is to be remembered, that they are more expoſed to

quick

quick Viciffitudes of Heat, Cold, Damps, and to various Changes of the Air and Weather, than moſt of the other Inhabitants in the Torrid Zone. Add to this, the Intemperance of Mariners, and the Exceſſes of every Kind which they are prone to fall into, whenever it is in their Power to commit them; all which render them more liable to Inflammations, than any other Set of People. Hence their Diſeaſes require more plentiful Evacuations than the Land Inhabitants in thoſe Parts of the World, and, generally, they bear them better.

This Rule alſo, as I before obſerved, does not take immediate Place in thoſe, who are newly arrived in the Torrid Zone. The unaccuſtomed Heat not only relaxes the Fibres, eſpecially at the Surface of the Body, but is found greatly to expand the Blood, and the other Fluids. A Proof of which, is, that young Perſons are often ſubject, upon their firſt Arrival, to an Hæmorrhage from the Noſe.

But with Regard to the Natives, or thoſe who have remained long in the Country, we grant the Uſage of Bleeding them but ſparingly to be extremely proper, making a ſmall Allowance for the different Seaſons of the Year,

Year, the Temperature of the Air, and the Situation of the Places where they reside. Thus, in some Parts, even on the Island of *Jamaica*, and at particular Seasons, the Weather is cool; wherefore, in these Places, and at such Seasons, the Inhabitants (having their Fibres more rigid, and a more compacted Blood) bear much better the Loss of that vital Fluid.

A very different and opposite Method to that of the *English*, is pursued by the *French*, but more especially by the *Spanish* and *Portuguese* Physicians in those Countries. The former bleed too freely, and have Recourse to the Operation in almost every acute Distemper; from whence leucophlegmatic and dropsical Diseases frequently ensue, the common and fatal Consequence of such Customs, and of profuse Evacuations in those Climates. The latter not only follow indiscriminately the Example of the former, in this Particular, but are solicitous to contrive the most cooling Remedies for all Diseases, whether acute, chronical, or what are commonly termed nervous. Whereas, in many Distempers classed under the two latter Denominations, warm, aromatic, invigorating Remedies ought, in sound Practice, to take Place, as much, if not more, in warm, than in colder Regions: And such Medicines are still more indisindifpenfably requifite in Weakneffes and Infirmity fucceeding acute Diforders.

In cold Countries, the State of the Air greatly affifts in reftoring the impaired Spring of the Fibres; whereas every thing almoft in warm Weather, fuch as Heat, Moifture, &c. concur to relax and weaken the Habit of Body. Thus, we may daily fee Perfons in *Britain*, after having fuffered a moft fevere Fit of Illnefs, recover their Strength and Spirits in a few Days, and, in a very fhort Time, their natural Conftitution. But the Cafe is very different in the fultry Regions of the Torrid Zone, or indeed in any Part of the World whatever, where the Heat of the Seafon raifes and fuftains the Mercury for a continued Time, at the 77th Degree and upwards, of *Fahrenheit*'s Thermometer. During fuch an Excefs of Heat, Debility after Fevers is apt to remain with *European* Conftitutions for feveral Months. In *Jamaica*, the Convalefcents are fent to the cool Summits of the Mountains; but often a Retreat to a more Northern Climate is abfolutely needful to recover their wonted Tone and Vigour of Body. It is an acknowledged Obfervation, that the *Negroes* and *Aborigines* in the Torrid Zone cannot bear too plentiful Evacuations by the Lancet.—They commonly mix the
moft

moſt ſtimulating, poignant Spices with their ordinary light Food, and this is experimentally found ſuitable to their Conſtitutions.

If indeed we may be allowed to aſſume it as a Principle, which Obſervation does in many Inſtances verify, that, in all Countries, Providence has wiſely ordered a Proviſion of the moſt proper Remedies for their peculiar and endemic Diſeaſes, we cannot here but remark, that moſt Part of the native medicinal Productions of the *Indies*, are of the warm aromatic Species; ſuch as Ginger, Contrayerva, Guajac, Winters-Bark, Pepper of many Kinds, and Spices almoſt of every Sort, together with Camphire, an excellent Medicine in hot Climates, and that grand Febrifuge, the *Peruvian* Bark, the moſt powerful Strengthener and Reſtorative of enfeebled, languid Conſtitutions, and the only Specific yet known for the malignant Diſeaſes of thoſe Climates.

SEVERAL Obſervations have been made of the different Degrees of Heat in various Latitudes, and the moſt accurate with *Fahrenheit*'s Thermometers.
But

But I have been furprized to find how much thofe Inftruments, though made by good Artifts, differed from each other. For which Reafon I have often thought that the comparative Quantities of Heat and Cold in different Places, would be beft afcertained by Obfervations made with the fame Inftrument. —I therefore fent the fame Thermometer abroad with careful Perfons; and by it meafured the Degrees of Heat and Cold from within 10 Degrees of the North Pole to *Jamaica*.

This Inftrument has been in my Poffeffion 14 Years; whofe erroneous printed Scale I was obliged to correct, fo as to fix the Point 32, by many repeated Experiments, precifely at the Degree of Cold, in which a Tea-cup full of Water begins in 5 Minutes to freeze when the Wind is dry and northerly. And I then found that there were but 23 Degrees of Tube left before the Mercury funk quite into the Ball: owing to a Fault of the Maker. I afterwards adjufted the Degrees afcending from 32, as nearly as I could by the boiling Water Heat of 212 Degrees; when the Mercury in the Barometer ftood in a middle Station.

According

According to this Correction of the Scale, I found 61 Degrees (that is 29 above the freezing Point) to be the usual and true Mean of agreeable warm Summer Weather in *England*, during the Months of *May* and *June*, and when a Fire in the Room was intolerable to People in Health.

54 was the usual Degree of Heat within Doors, in the warmest Days of Winter; and then I could either read or write in my Study, without a Fire: but when the Temperature of the Air was under 54, a Fire became requisite.

The lowest, in six Years Observations, I found the Mercury ever to sink at *Edinburgh*, during the severest Frosts, and when exposed all Night out of a north Window, in the open Air, was to 23 Degrees, on the 3d *February*, 1757. But in most Winters it seldom fell lower than 25 or 24 Degrees, and it was then intensely cold.

The severest Cold experienced in four Winters at *Haslar* Hospital, was on the 14th *January*, 1760. On that Day the Mercury within Doors fell to 29 Degrees: Water at this Time freezing hard when kept in the same Room.

The

The Instrument being placed in the open Air, that Night at 12 o'Clock, it stood at 22 Degrees; which was the lowest I ever observed. And at this Time the Sea-Water stagnating in Ponds, became covered with thin Ice.

During the Years 1758, 1759 and 1761, there was no such extraordinary Degree of Cold at *Haslar*, the greatest being 25 or 26.

At *Edinburgh*, the warmest Weather in *June*, *July*, and *August*, was commonly 70 in the Middle of the Day, and 64 in the Night. But during uncommon Heats, the Mercury has risen to 73 and 75, perhaps once or twice in a Year, and sometimes not in two Years. The greatest Heat observed by the Instrument there was on the 12th *July*, 1757, when in the Middle of the Day, and well shaded, it mounted to 80 Degrees. The Heat was then quite stifling.

At *Haslar* I found the usual Heats in Summer about 2 Degrees higher than at *Edinburgh*. The hottest Day I ever felt here was 22 *July*, 1759, when the Instrument at Noon, in the open Air, mounted to 81 Degrees, and the Temperature of my Room, with all the Windows

dows and Doors open till 10 o'Clock at Night was 75.

Many *West Indians* thought the Heat this Day as great as they had felt in the *West Indies*. At Noon there was no fitting in a Room without having all the Windows open, and a Shade from the Sun.

The fame Inftrument, from which thofe Obfervations were taken, was fent to *Greenland* with Mr. *Rannie*, now Surgeon of a Man of War; and in the Latitude of 80, the Mercury funk quite into the Ball, fo muft have fallen to 9 Degrees, but how much below that cannot be afcertained. Now fuppofing it to have fallen only to 9, then the Cold in that Latitude furpaffed the moft fevere Froft that I had obferved at *Edinburgh* or *Haflar* by 13 Degrees. And as with the hardeft Froft in *Great Britain*, I never faw the Mercury fall lower than 10 Degrees under the Point, at which Water freezes; there it fell 23 Degrees below it.

When the *Greenland* Ship was in more fouthern Latitudes, but ftill among the Ice; the Inftrument in the great Cabbin ftood at 31, and when brought upon Deck fell to 25 or 22 Degrees: which was the common Temperature

ture of the Air during the Summer in that icy Sea, when the Sun did not shine forth.

The same Thermometer, in the Year 1752, was sent to *Jamaica* with a judicious Person, who touched at *Cork* in *Ireland*, and made the following Observations: The Instrument being placed on the outside of the Cabbin Window, and secured both from the direct and reflected Rays of the Sun.

	Degrees highest.	Lowest.	Mean or common Heat.
From *Cork* Lat. 51 : 49 20 *Jan.* to Lat. 41 : 44 27 *Jan.*	58	46	54
to Lat. 31 : 40 1 *Feb.*	64	54	59
to Lat. 21 : 40 7 *Feb.*	72	61	63
to Lat. 16 : 40 13 *Feb.*	77	67	72
Keeping in Lat. 16 : 40 to 24 *Feb.* when the Ship arrived at *Jamaica*	81	74	77

In *Port Royal* Harbour on the 24th of *February*, and for some Days following, till the Observer fell sick, the common Heat of the Day was 79 or 80 Degrees,

In the Year 1761 this Thermometer was sent in the *Stag* Man of War to the Streights of *Gibraltar*.

The lowest it ever fell there on Ship-board, during the Months of *June* and *July*, in which

which the Obfervations were taken, was on the 20th of *June* in *Gibraltar* Bay to 64; and the loweft at Land was on the 12th of *June* in *Gibraltar* at 73.

The higheft it ever rofe on the faireft Trials in the Shade, was the 4th of *July*, at *Oran* in *Africa*, to 86; and at *Gibraltar* on the 16th of the fame Month, to 90. But the higheft Degree it ever reached on board the Ship was 78. —And by feveral accurate Obfervations it appeared that the Heat at Land in *Gibraltar* exceeded that in the Ship upon the Water, by 8 or 10 Degrees; and at *Oran* by 6; and that the common Heat during Summer in the Garrifon of *Gibraltar* is from 79 to 87 Degrees.

From thefe Accounts it appears that the Heat in *Gibraltar*, on the 16th of *July*, exceeded the moft extraordinary Heat felt in *England* for 14 Years paft, 9 Degrees;—and that the ufual Summer Heat there exceeds that of *Britain* 15 or 17 Degrees.

But the higheft the Mercury ever rofe on the Water in *Gibraltar* Bay, in *June* and *July*, was to 78; and the common Heat on the Water in *Port Royal* Harbour in *February* being 79 or 80; hence the Summer Heat in *Gi-*

braltar Bay was not quite so much as in the Month of *February* in *Port Royal* Harbour. Tho' perhaps the Heat on Shore at *Jamaica*, in the Winter Month of *February*, was nearly equal to the Summer's Heat at *Gibraltar*.

By perusing a very exact thermometrical Diary, kept in the *Montague* Man of War, when in the *West Indies*, and adjusting the Instrument to the corrected Scale of my Thermometer, I found that from *May* 24, to *August* 25, *Anno*, 1760, the Heat in the open Gallery of that Ship had never been less than 75 Degrees, nor exceeded 88; and if we allow 6 Degrees of greater Heat at Land in *Barbadoes, Antigua, Guadalupe, &c.* where the Ship was stationed, the greatest Summer Heat in those Islands will be 94 Degrees, which approaches to within 2 Degrees of the Warmth of the vital Blood, which circulates thro' the Heart of a Man in Health.—And to this Temperature, the Water, as also all other Fluids, together with the Earth, and all the Solids, in those *West Indian* Islands, were then heated when in the Shade, *viz.* 62 Degrees above the Cold with which Water becomes a Solid, or is converted into Ice, and 118 Degrees below the Heat of boiling Water, exceeding the greatest Heat experienced by my Thermometer in *Britain*, for 14 Years past, by 13 Degrees.

POST-

POSTSCRIPT.

AS some have imagined the Diseases of Seamen to be different from those who live at Land, I have here subjoined an Abstract of the Distempers of all such Mariners as have been received into *Haslar* Hospital for two Years, *viz.* from the first of July 1758, to the first of July 1760; the Number of such Patients being 5743. Of these, 2174 were afflicted with *Fevers*, 1146 with *Scurvies*, 360 with *Consumptions**, 350 with *Rheumatisms*, 245 with the *Dysentery*, and other *Fluxes* of the

---

* Of these 360 consumptive Patients, the Disease in one fourth of them was owing to a Cause well deserving Attention. It proceeded from Falls, Bruises, Strains, or Hurts affecting the Trunk of the Body, and which often gave no great Uneasiness for one Year, or perhaps two; and the Cause lay concealed till after Death, when in the bruised

the Belly, acute and chronical. These are by far the most frequent and fatal Diseases in the Royal Navy. Besides which, seafaring People are subject to other common Maladies. During those two Years, there were also received 10 for the *Angina*, three for the *Apoplexy*, 40 for the *Asthma*, 67 for the *Ague* or *intermit-*

bruised or hurt Part (either within or without the Cavity of the Breast) I often found large Collections of Matter in Bags; at other Times the Parts were *scirrhous* and always diseased For a Cough, with other concomitant consumptive Symptoms, as I have discovered by Dissection, does not always argue the Mischief to lie in the Breast, but are the Signs of a weakened, drooping and wasting Habit.

Daily viewing so many piteous consumptive Objects, I have often reflected on the Barbarity of severe Cudgel-playing, Boxing and Bruising among the Vulgar; as also beating on the Trunk of the Body with a heavy Stick; where, tho' the Smart of the Blow soon ceases, a Foundation is often laid for an inward Malady, becoming mortal some Years afterwards, of which I have seen many Instances.

The Death of a Prince of amiable Memory, is said to have been owing to the violent Stroke of a Tennis-Ball; which gave no great Uneasiness for some Time after received.

Let it be remembered, that the human Machine is of too delicate a Texture, to bear rude Shocks or Bruises; and that the Injuries of its inward solid Parts are the most irreparable.

ting

ting Fever, 80 for Complaints of old Hurts, *&c.* 20 *Chachectic*, five for the *Chincough*, 10 for *Colics*, 24 for the *Dropsy*, six for *Deafness*, 30 for the *Epilepsy*, 30 for various Disorders of the *Eyes*, three for the true *Gout*, 20 for the *Gravel*, 17 for *chronic Head-achs*, 30 for *Spitting of Blood*, 10 *Hypochondriac*, 15 for the *Jaundice*, 25 for *Incontinency of Urine* *, 3 for the *Lethargy*, 7 for the *Lientery*, 30 for the *Leprosy*, 20 for the *Lumbago*, 14 for *Madness*, 5 for *Melancholy*, 31 for the *Measles*, 20 for the *Palsy*, 29 for the *true Peripneumony*, 11 for the *true Pleurisy*, 73 for *cutaneous Diseases*, seven for the *Sciatick*, 53 for the *Small-pox*, five for the *Strangury*, 15 for the *Scrofula*, 20 for *Scalled-Heads*. There remain 680 Patients, whose Cases are not here mentioned, having been chiefly *Surgical*, *Venereal*, the *Itch*, or feigned Complaints.

* This is often a Complaint feigned by Seamen, at other Times it proceeds from Falls or Bruises.

The E N D.

Formulæ medicamentorum facilium paratu, atque in morbis nauticis apprimé utilium.

FEBRIS. ℞ *Sal. nitri unc. ii. cremor. Tartari, unc. iii. M. terantur in pulverem. Dos. drach. ſs. ſextâ quaque horâ.* ℞ *Teſt. oſtreorum præp. (ſeu cretæ alb. præp.) unc. ii. cremor. Tartari, unc. i. M. fiat pulvis. Dos. drach. ſs. ſextâ quaque horâ.* ℞ *Sal. Tartari, unc. i. Cremor. Tartari, unc. ii. Diligenter ſimul in pulverem terantur. Dos drach. ſs. ſæpius in die.* ℞ *Aquæ hordeatæ, lib. ii. cui adde pro re nata ſal. nitri drach. i. — vel oxymel. ſimp. unc. i ſs. — vel gum. arabici unc. ſs. — vel elixir vitrioli acid. drach. i. — vel ſpir. vitrioli fort. ſcrup. ſs. Sit pro potu uſitato.* ℞ *Aquæ hordeatæ lib. ii. Cremor. Tartari drach. i. coque ad ſolutionem uſque Tartari, et decoƈto ſubſidentiâ depurato adde ſyr. e ſucc. limonum unc. i. Sit pro pota aſſiduo.* ℞ *Aquæ puræ lib. vii. ſpiritûs vinoſi tenuioris lib. i. ſacchari albi unc. iv. M. Fiat julepum commune.* ℞ *Julepi commun. unc. vi. cui adde pro re nata Tartari emetic. a gr. i. ad gr. iii. — vel vini antimon. a drach. i. ad drach. iii. — vel ſpirit. nitri dulcis drach. ii. — vel ſpirit. vitrioli dulcis drach. i. — vel vini crocei unc. ſs. — vel ſal. nitri ſcrup. ii. vel ſal.*

U *diuretici*

diuretici drach. i. — vel moschi (cum saccharo triti) a scrup. i. ad scrup. ii. — vel sal. cornu cervi (omisso spir. vinos. ten.) scrup. i. Dos. unc. i. quartâ vel sextâ quaque horâ. ℞ *Camphoræ drach. i. mucilag. gum. Arabici drach. v. probe subigantur, Dos. gr. xxv. quartâ vel sexta quaque horâ.* ℞ *Rob. limonum sal. Tartari (vel Absinthii) āā drach. i. aquæ puræ unc. iv. tinct. cinnamomi drach. vi. syrup. simp. unc. ss. M. et adde pro re nata Mithridatii a drach. ss. ad drach. i ss. — vel elect. e scordio drach. i ss. aut drach. ii. — vel spirit. lavendulæ comp. drach. ii. — vel elixir. paregoric. drach. i ss. Dos. ab unc. i. ad unc. i ss.* ℞ *Cortic. Peruviani triti unc. i. vel unc. i ss. aquæ puræ lib. iv. coquantur ad lib. i ss. injiciendo paulò ante finem cocturæ gum. Arabici drach. i. Colaturæ adde pro re nata tinct. cort. Peruviani simp. lib. ss. — vel sal. nitri drach. i. — vel elixir. vitriol. acid. drach. i ss. — vel vini crocei aut tincturæ Thebaicæ q. s. Dos. ab unc. ii. ad unc. iii. ter quaterve die.*

Febris intermittens. ℞ *Cort. Peruviani pulv. unc. i. syr. e cort. aurantiorum, q. s. M. f. electarium. Adde pro re nata pulv. rhabarbari scrup. ii. — vel pulv. cort. cascarillæ unc. ss. — vel pulv. nucis moschatæ, aluminis rupei āā drach. ii. — vel sal. ammoniaci pur. drach. i. — vel rubig. chalybis præp. drach. ii.* ℞ *Herb. absinthii roman. drach. iii. Cort. aurantiorum siccat. drach. i. Aquæ puræ unc. xviii. coque parum ad lib.*

lib. i. Colaturæ adde pro re nata sal. Tartari (vel sal. absinthii) scrup. iv. — vel tinct. cort. Peruviani simp. unc. iv. — vel sal. ammoniaci pur. scrup. ii. Dos. unc. iv. ter die.

Scorbutus. ℞ Rob. limonum drach. iii. sacchari unc. ii. optimè commixtis adde vini albi hispan. lib. i. Dos. ab unc. ss. ad unc. ii. quartâ quaque horâ, quo tempore agitetur lagena ut lenis excitetur fermentatio. Fit quoque in vicem rob. substituendo suc. limonum unc. v. — vel suc. aurantiorum unc. vi. ℞ Summit. pini Anglicè dictæ hemlock pine Gallicè la prusse, sive epinette blanche lib. i. optimè contusis in mortario affunde aq. puræ tepid. lib. viii. macera in vase clauso, subinde agitans, per 12 horas in loco tepido, et cola. Dos. lib. ss. mane et hora decubitûs, vel ad lib. ii. per diem. ℞ Conserv. absinthii maritim. elect. lenitivi āā p. æ. elixir. vitriol. acid. q. s. ad acerrimum saporem. Dos. drach. i. bis die. ℞ Summit. absinthii maritim. manipul. i. cerevisiæ tenuis cong. i. macera per biduum pro potu assiduo. ℞ Pulv. subt. cort. Peruviani drach. ss. syr. e succo limonum. q. s. f. bolus bis per diem sumendus.

Phthisis. ℞ Spermat. ceti (cum mucilag. gum. Arabici subact.) drach. iii. aquæ puræ unc. vii. tinct. cinnamomi syrupi simp. āā unc. i. M. Adde pro re nata sal. nitri drach. i. — vel lac ammoniaci unc. ii. — vel syr. scillitici unc. ss. — vel elixir. paregoric. unc. ss. — vel sal. cornu cervi drach. ss. Dos unc. i. sexta quaque hora. ℞ Furfuris manipul. i. aquæ puræ lib. iv. coquantur ad lib. ii. colaturæ adde mellis despumat. unc. i. M. pro potu assiduo. ℞ Olei olivarum syr. balsamic. āā unc. i. mucilag. gum. Arabici unc. ss. M. f. Lohoch, additis non-nunquam spir. vitrioli tenuis gutt. xii. Detur cochleare parvulum subinde vexante ussi. ℞ Infusi amar. simp. lib. ss. tinct. cort. Peruviani simp. drach. vi. elixir. vitrioli drach. ss. M. Dos. unc. ii. ter in die. ℞ Calomel. gr. v. pulv. rhabarbari scrup. ss. confect. cardiac. q. s. f. bolus matutinus. ℞ Aq. puræ unc. i ss. tinct. cardamomi syr. e meconio āā drach. ii. tinct. thebaicæ a gutt. xx. ad xxx. lixiv. Tartari drach. ss. M. f. haustus vespertinus.

Rheumatismus Chronicus. ℞ Saponis Hispan. unc. iii. mellis unc. ii. M. f. electarium. Adde pro re nata cinnabar. antimonii unc. i ss. — vel flor. sulphuris unc. i. — vel gum. guaiaci unc. i. — vel gum. ammoniaci drach. vi. — vel ol. essential. e baccis juniperi drach. iii. — vel pulv. scillæ exsiccat. drach. i ss. syr. e corticib. aurantior. (interdum e meconio) q. s. f. elect. Dos scrup. ii. bis in die. Medicamenta Varia. Tinct. guaiacina volatilis; a gutt. xx. ad drach. ii. ol. terebinthinæ æther. ad gutt. lx. bis die.
Sal.

Sal prunellæ, ad drach. ſs. bis die. balſ. guaiacinum, ad gutt. xxx. bis die. vin. antimoniale, a gutt. xii. ad drach. i ſs. Tartarum emeticum ad gran. ſs. ter in die. Antimonium præp. ad drach. ſs. bis die. Ol. eſſential. e ſeminib. aniſi, ad gutt. xl. Aq. calcis ſimp. ad lib. i. per diem. Aqua picea, ad unc. iv. ter in die. Sem. ſinapi integra, ad cochleare unum ſive unc. ſs. bis de die. Pſychroluſia, ſeu immerſio in aqua marina.

Diarrhœa Dyſenteria. *Pulv. ipecacuanhæ, a gr. v. ad ſcrup. i. — Rad. rhabarbari, a gr. x. ad drach. i. — Vitr. antimonii cerat. gr. v. — Calomel, gr. v. — Pilulæ ſaponaceæ, a gr. v. ad ſcrup. ſs.* ℞ *Elect. e ſcordio drach. ſs. f. bolus addantur pro re nata pulv. rhabarbari drach. ſs. — vel rhabarb. torrefact. gr. xv. — vel pulv. ipecacuanh. gr. i. M.* ℞ *Spec. e ſcordio ſine opio ſcrup. ſs. Philon. Lond. gr. vii. ſyr. e meconio, q. ſ. f. Bolus poſt ſingulas ſedes repetendus.* ℞ *Capit. papaver. alb. contus. unc. ſs. cort. Peruviani trit. unc. i ſs. aquæ puræ lib. iv. coque ad lib. ii. ſub finem injiciendo gum. Arabici cinnamomi āā drach. i. colaturæ fortiter expreſſæ detur unc. i. omni bihorio, additis ſi res poſtulat elixir. paregor. guttis aliquot.* ℞ *Aq. hordeat. unc. vi. vel iv. mucilag. gum Arabici unc. ſs. vel drach. ii. M. f. enema. Adde pro re nata tinct. thebaic. gutt. xl. — vel elect. e ſcordio drach. ii. — vel vini rubri unc. ii. — vel decoct. Peruvian.*

Peruvian. modo præscrip. unc. ii. ℞ Cort. quercus drach. vi. coq. ex aq. pur. lib. iii. ad lib. ii. injiciendo sub finem coctionis flor: rosarum rubr. drach. ii. colaturæ adde tinct. cinnamomi unc. ii. tinct. japonicæ unc. i. detur lib. i. per diem. ℞ Aq. calcis simp. lib. i. syr. balsamic. (vel e meconio) unc. i. M. Dos. unc. ii. aut iii. ter die.

Colica Pictonum, Anglicè dry belly-ach. ℞ Pulv. ipecacuanhæ gr. xii. Tartari emetic. gr. i. M. f. pulvis emeticus si opus sit, interdum exhibendus. ℞ Rob. limonum, sal. absinthii āā scrup. i. aq. menthæ spirit. unc. i ss. opii puri gr. i. vel gr. i ss. syr. e meconio drach. i. M. S. A. f. Haustus pro re nata sumendus. ℞ Extracti cathartici gr. xv. vel drach. ss. calomel. gr. x. opii puri gr. i ss. saponis alb. gr. vi. ol. essent. menthæ vulg. gutt. ii. syr. e corticib. aurantior. q. s. Cogantur in massam pilularem S. A. in pilulas gr. vi. dividendam pro dosi una. ℞ Infusi senæ commun. unc. iii. tinct. senæ drach. iii. olei olivarum opt. unc. ss. syr. e meconio drach. ii. M. f. potio purgans. Detur unc. i. quoque bihorio, post exhibitionem pilular. modo præscript. utatur æger semicupio. ℞ Capit. papaveris alb. drach. iii. aq. puræ lib. i ss. coq. ad unc. x. injiciendo sub finem cocturæ flor. chamæmeli drach. ii. Colaturæ fortiter expressæ adde ol. olivarum unc. ii. saponis alb. unc. ss. M. f. enema. ℞ Calomel. gr. i. camphoræ gr. vi. Bals. Peruviani q. s. f. pilulæ duæ bis in die repetendæ.

ERRATA.

Page 28. line 8. for *principle*, read *principal*. Pag. 35. line 11. for *where*, read *when*. Pag. 45. line penult. for *Madegascar*, read *Madagascar*. Pag. 65. line 21. for *it*, read *its*. Pag. 74. line ult. for *Porea*, read *Portsea*. Pag. 80. line 4. et ult. for *Cape Corsa*, read *Cape Corso*. Pag. 85. for *Mr. Robinson*, read *Mr. Robertson*. Pag. 88. line 6. for *pipe filled*, read *pipe fitted*. Pag. 91. line ult. for *when thawed*, read *when alternately thawed, and froze again in different sea-water*.

www.ingramcontent.com/pod-product-compliance
Lightning Source LLC
Chambersburg PA
CBHW032158160426
43197CB00008B/968